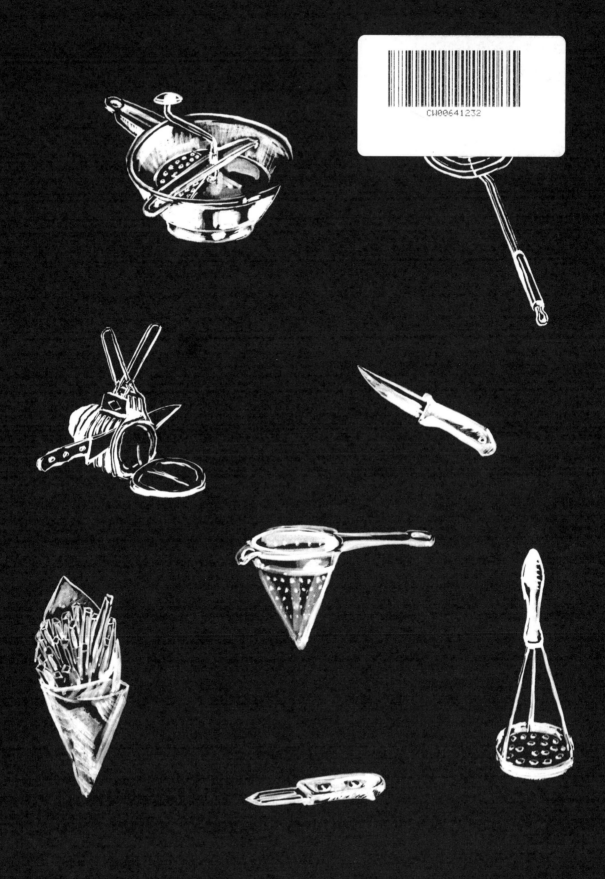

Beef & Potatoes

Beef & Potatoes

200 recipes for the perfect steak
and chips, and so much more

Jean-François Mallet

MURDOCH BOOKS

SYDNEY · LONDON

Introduction

All my uncle eats is steak and chips. Whether he is in Italy, China or Thailand, that's all he chooses to eat. And my uncle is no philistine – he is a Frenchman who lives in the area around Lyon, the capital of good eating.

Is it shameful to be a devotee of steak and chips in the land of high gastronomy? Absolutely not, because not just anyone can make it well. Sure, it is on the menu of every brasserie and on the chalkboard of every bistro in France, but quite often it is an impostor. You are served poor meat badly cooked and potatoes that taste only of oil. Whereas a good steak and chips, well, the devotees are right – there is nothing better. And perhaps this is all they eat because they are on a quest to find the perfect version.

Steak and chips is so good, and so difficult to do well, that one day the great chef Michel Troisgros said to us, after a photo shoot and interview: 'Sit down, I will make you something to eat.' We expected a lobster thermidor, an iced wild green soup with chicken oysters… Nothing of the sort! He came back with an unforgettable fillet steak with soufflé potatoes.

Steak and chips is a sort of metonymy – the quintessential form of beef and potatoes – but there are infinite variations on the formula. To throw people off the scent, so to speak, all you have to do is firmly declare that you are not difficult to please, the proof being you eat everything: classic cottage pie; beef wellington with duchess potatoes; beef and potato croquettes; (good) steak and chips… As long as there are meat and potatoes, you're happy. Take your pick!

BEEF

BEEF

The simplistic soul who just thinks 'beef' without considering which cut or chooses only T-bone steak time and again (and everything else goes into the mincer) has no hope. If he wants a slow-cooked stew and chooses the wrong cut, he will find himself with shoe leather. If he wants to barbecue and chooses boiling beef, he will be stuck with rubbery meat. The whole point of butchery is to precisely identify the right cut for each way of cooking.

Suddenly it all becomes clear – choosing which bit of the cow to use is no small matter, because cooking beef is an art in itself. And since an encyclopedia wouldn't be enough if you wanted to go into the details, let's stick to the basics. The front parts, which contain a lot of sinew, require slow cooking (braising, stewing, roasting), because the sinew turns into collagen and provides gelatine. The back parts lend themselves to quick cooking methods (grilling, pan-frying). The better quality the meat, the more cuts (back or front) you can grill or pan-fry successfully. Meats of lesser quality are more suited to slow cooking because they are tougher. As for the rest, your butcher is your best guide.

MARINATED AND GRILLED RIB STEAK

Serves 4–6

4 sprigs thyme, plus extra
to serve

1 sprig rosemary, plus
extra to serve

2 bay leaves

250 g (9 oz) cherry
tomatoes

8 pink garlic cloves (or
white if not available)

200 ml (7 fl oz)
olive oil

1 large rib steak
(about 2.5 kg/5 lb 8 oz)

Preparation time
10 minutes

Cooking time
20 minutes

Resting time
Overnight

Meat resting time
5 minutes

Wash, dry and roughly chop the herbs. Cut the cherry tomatoes in half and bruise the garlic cloves in their skin.

Heat the oil in a small saucepan over low heat. Add the garlic cloves and let them cook for 10 minutes over very low heat. Check they are cooked by inserting the tip of a knife. Remove the saucepan from the heat and let the garlic cool a little. Add the herbs and tomatoes. Set aside to let the oil infuse and cool completely.

Lightly trim the rib steak of excess fat and place in a large, deep dish. Drain the garlic cloves, herbs and tomatoes, put into a bowl, cover and set aside in the refrigerator. Use the oil to coat the steak. Cover with plastic wrap and let the steak marinate overnight in the refrigerator.

The next day, at serving time, drain the rib steak on a plate. Season with salt and pepper, then cook on a preheated hot barbecue, or in an oven preheated to 180°C (350°F), or in a frying pan over high heat for about 5 minutes each side. Cover with foil to keep the steak warm and let it rest for 5 minutes, turning it over once.

Serve with the reserved garlic, cherry tomatoes and herbs.

Suggestion
Serve the rib steak with sautéed potatoes with olives and basil (p. 282), oven-baked skin-on chips (p. 298) or barbecued potatoes with rosemary oil (p. 300).

SAUTÉED BEEF WITH MUSHROOMS

Serves 4

300 g (10½ oz) button mushrooms

700 g (1 lb 9 oz) beef for pan-frying (inside round, rump, tenderloin or striploin)

2 pink garlic cloves (or white if not available)

4 tablespoons olive oil

3 sprigs thyme

2 bay leaves

4 tablespoons sherry vinegar

Preparation time
25 minutes

Cooking time
10 minutes

Wash, de-stem and slice the mushrooms. Cut the meat into small, thin slices. Peel and thinly slice the garlic cloves.

Heat 2 tablespoons oil in a large frying pan over high heat. Add the mushrooms to the hot oil and cook until browned (if they release any liquid, reduce it in the pan until it has completely evaporated). Set them aside on a plate.

Wipe out the frying pan and heat the remaing oil over high heat. Add the pieces of beef and garlic to the hot oil and cook for 2 minutes, or until browned. Add the thyme and bay leaves. Add the vinegar and boil, stirring, for 30 seconds to deglaze the pan. Add the mushrooms, stir through and transfer the contents of the pan to a serving plate.

Suggestion
Serve immediately with potato purée (p. 254).

BEEF, CAPSICUM AND ANCHOVY SKEWERS

Serves 4
700 g (1 lb 9 oz)
rump steak

4 garlic cloves

12 anchovy fillets in oil

4 tablespoons
soy sauce

2 red capsicums (peppers)

2 tablespoons olive oil

Special equipment
Small skewers

Preparation time
25 minutes

Cooking time
5 minutes

Resting time
3 hours

If using wooden skewers, soak them in water until ready to use.

Cut the rump steak into cubes of a similar size, about 2.5 cm (1 inch). Peel the garlic cloves, then finely chop or crush. Cut the anchovy fillets in half.

Combine the garlic, anchovies and soy sauce in a medium bowl. Add the cubed beef, cover with plastic wrap and marinate for 3 hours in the refrigerator.

Remove the stem and insides of the capsicums, then cut the flesh into small pieces.

Heat the olive oil in a large frying pan over high heat. Add the capsicum and cook for 2–3 minutes, or until browned. Remove from the heat and set aside to cool.

Assemble 12 small skewers, threading on alternating pieces of meat (reserving the marinade), anchovy and capsicum.

Preheat the barbecue or a frying pan to medium–high. Cook the skewers, turning, for 5 minutes, or until the beef is rare or cooked to your liking. Arrange the skewers on a serving plate.

Suggestion
Serve these skewers with sautéed potatoes with olives and basil (p. 282).

CLASSIC HAMBURGERS

Makes 4 hamburgers
8 lettuce leaves of choice

4 gherkins (pickles)

2 large tomatoes

1 red onion

700 g (1 lb 9 oz) minced (ground) beef

2 tablespoons olive oil

4 hamburger buns

4 tablespoons mayonnaise

4 slices emmental cheese

4 tablespoons mustard

Special equipment
Small wooden skewers

Preparation time
30 minutes

Cooking time
10 minutes

Wash and dry the lettuce leaves. Slice the gherkins lengthways and slice the tomatoes and onion into rounds.

Preheat the oven to 180°C (350°F). Season the meat with salt and pepper and knead it well. Shape into 4 large and fairly thick patties of equal size.

Heat the oil in a large frying pan over high heat. Cook the meat patties for 3 minutes on each side, or until browned and cooked through.

Split open the buns and toast them in the oven for 5 minutes. Brush each of the bottom halves with 1 tablespoon mayonnaise, then add the lettuce, meat patties, cheese, rounds of tomato and onion, and gherkin slices. Brush each of the top halves of the buns with 1 tablespoon mustard, place on top of the fillings. Press the burger down lightly and hold in place with a wooden skewer.

Suggestion
Serve immediately with crispy potato chips (p. 238).

RIB EYE STEAK WITH RED WINE SAUCE

Serves 4

4 large rib eye (entrecôte) steaks, about 200 g (7 oz) each

2 tablespoons sunflower oil

50 g (1¾ oz) butter

1 garlic clove

For the sauce

5 French shallots

1 tablespoon olive oil

135 g (4¾ oz) butter

1 sprig thyme

2 bay leaves

1 teaspoon raw (demerara) sugar

500 ml (17 fl oz/2 cups) red wine (cabernet merlot or bordeaux blend)

250 ml (9 fl oz/1 cup) brown veal stock

Preparation time

25 minutes

Cooking time

15 minutes (meat)

45 minutes (sauce)

To make the red wine sauce, peel and slice the shallots. Heat the olive oil and 50 g (1¾ oz) butter in a small saucepan over medium–high heat. Add the shallots and cook for 2 minutes. Add the thyme, bay leaves and sugar, then reduce the heat to low and let the shallots soften and caramelise for 10 minutes, stirring with a wooden spoon occasionally.

Pour in the wine and boil, stirring, for 30 seconds to deglaze the pan. Allow the liquid to reduce by a quarter, then add the stock and reduce by half, still over a low heat. Taste the sauce and season with salt and pepper. Add 80 g (2¾ oz) butter and whisk constantly, not letting the sauce come back to the boil. Set aside in a bain-marie (water bath).

Around 10 minutes before serving time, season the steaks with salt and pepper. Heat the oil and butter in a large frying pan over high heat. Add the steaks and garlic clove, bruised in its skin, to the pan and cook for 3 minutes on each side, basting regularly with the cooking juices. Arrange the steaks on large plates and pour a generous amount of the sauce over.

Suggestion

Serve with crispy potato chips (p. 238) or sautéed potatoes with olives and basil (p. 282).

FILLET STEAK WITH TRUFFLES AND FOIE GRAS

Serves 4

1 small tin (25 g/1 oz) truffle slices

1 tablespoon sweet madeira (or sweet sherry or muscat)

50 g (1¾ oz) butter

1 tablespoon sunflower oil

4 thick beef tenderloin (fillet) steaks, about 190 g (6¾ oz each)

300 g (10½ oz) foie gras

Fine sea salt

Freshly ground black pepper

Special equipment
Whisk

Foil

Preparation time
15 minutes

Cooking time
20 minutes

Meat resting time
5 minutes

Drain the truffle slices, reserving the liquid, and set them aside. Pour the truffle liquid and madeira into a small saucepan over medium–high heat. Bring to the boil, then remove from the heat and add the butter, whisking continuously. Season with fine sea salt and freshly ground black pepper, and set aside in a bain-marie (water bath) without letting it boil.

Heat the oil in a large frying pan over high heat. Season the steaks, add to the pan and cook for 4 minutes on each side. Drain the steaks, put them on a plate and cover with foil. Let the steaks rest for 5 minutes, turning them over once.

Wipe out the frying pan and place over very high heat. Cut the foie gras into slices, season with fine sea salt and freshly ground black pepper, and add to the very hot dry frying pan. Brown the foie gras slices for a few seconds on each side, then transfer to a plate.

Place the steaks on serving plates, top each with a slice of foie gras, pour a little truffle butter over and garnish with the truffle slices.

Suggestion
Serve this dish with potato purée (see p. 254) and carrot or pumpkin purée.

COLD BEEF PICNIC PIES

Serves 4

For the filling
200 g (7 oz) pork belly

1 teaspoon fine sea salt

¼ teaspoon freshly ground black pepper

1 teaspoon thyme leaves

1 tablespoon whisky

700 g (1 lb 9 oz) minced (ground) beef

For the pastry
500 g (1 lb 2 oz) plain (all-purpose) flour

1 teaspoon fine sea salt

150 g (5½ oz) lard

2 eggs

1 egg yolk

Special equipment
Food processor

Preparation time
45 minutes

Resting time
1 hour

Cooking time
45 minutes

Cut the pork belly into small pieces and process it with the salt, pepper and thyme until fine. Transfer the mixture to a bowl, add the whisky and minced beef and mix together. Cover with plastic wrap and marinate in the refrigerator for 1 hour.

Meanwhile, to make the pastry, combine the flour and salt in a medium bowl. Dissolve the lard in a little water, add to the flour mixture and stir to combine. Add the eggs, one at a time, and mix vigorously after each addition to make a smooth dough.

Preheat the oven to 180°C (350°F). Roll out 4 circles of pastry, each about 12 cm (4½ inches) across, and press them into 4 ramekins to line the bottom and side. Fill with the meat mixture, packing it down well. Roll out the remaining pastry and cut out 4 small circles. Top the pies with the pastry rounds and press the edges of the base and top together with your fingertips to seal. Make a small hole in the middle of the pastry tops with the tip of a knife. Carefully remove the pies from the ramekins and brush them with the beaten egg yolk.

Place the pies on a baking tray and bake for 45 minutes, or until golden and cooked through. Set them aside to cool and then pack and serve them with grapes or fresh figs and a green salad.

BEEF BOURGUIGNON

Serves 4–6

100 ml (3½ fl oz) sunflower oil

1.5 kg stewing beef (blade, chuck or shin), cut into large cubes

450 g (1 lb) bacon or speck, diced

1 large sprig thyme

2 bay leaves

1 tablespoon plain (all-purpose) flour

1 litre (35 fl oz/4 cups) red wine (burgundy or pinot noir)

500 ml (17 fl oz/2 cups) brown veal stock

250 g (9 oz) baby onions

250 g (9 oz) small mushrooms

80 g (2¾ oz) butter

1 teaspoon caster (superfine) sugar

Special equipment
Large cast-iron casserole dish

Preparation time
25 minutes

Cooking time
About 2 hours

Heat 3 tablespoons of the oil in the casserole dish over medium–high heat. Add the beef and cook until browned on all sides. Add 200 g (7 oz) of the bacon with the thyme, bay leaves and flour. Mix together and cook for 5 minutes, or until browned. Add the wine and cook until reduced. Add the stock and season with salt and pepper. Reduce the heat to medium–low, cover the dish halfway with a lid and simmer for at least 2 hours, keeping the casserole dish half-covered so the liquid doesn't evaporate too quickly.

Meanwhile, peel the onions and set aside. De-stem, wash and dry the mushrooms. Heat 1 tablespoon of the oil in a frying pan over medium–high heat. Add the mushrooms and cook until browned. Set aside.

Put 50 g (1¾ oz) of the butter and the remaining 1 tablespoon of oil in a large, deep frying pan over medium–high heat. When the butter has melted, add the onions and cook until browned. Add the sugar and cook, stirring, until the onions have caramelised. Add 50 ml (1½ fl oz) water and boil, stirring, for 30 seconds to deglaze the pan. When the liquid has evaporated, lower the heat to medium and add the remaining bacon. Cook gently for 15 minutes, stirring from time to time. Add the mushrooms and the remaining butter. Season with salt and pepper.

At serving time, add the bacon and onion mixture to the casserole dish, stir through and bring to the boil. Season with salt and pepper to taste and place the casserole dish directly on the table. Serve with steamed potatoes.

Suggestion
A bourguignon is even better made the day before and reheated. Spread the word!

T-BONE STEAK WITH SPECIAL SAUCE

Serves 4–6

1 white onion

2 garlic cloves

½ red capsicum (pepper)

3 tablespoons
sunflower oil

4 tablespoons honey

4 tablespoons
tomato sauce (ketchup)

50 ml (1½ fl oz) red wine

1 tablespoon tomato paste
(concentrated purée)

3 cloves

1 T-bone steak, about
1.2 kg/2 lb 11 oz
(or 2 smaller ones)

Special equipment
Food processor
(or stick blender)

Preparation time
25 minutes

Cooking time
2 hours 30 minutes

Meat resting time
5–6 minutes

Peel and chop the onion and garlic. Finely dice the capsicum. Heat 1 tablespoon of the sunflower oil in a saucepan over medium heat. Add the onion, garlic and capsicum and cook gently, stirring, until lightly browned. Add the honey and allow the mixture to caramelise. Add the tomato sauce, wine and tomato paste and stir through.

Reduce the heat to low, add the cloves, and cook gently, stirring from time to time, until the sauce is reduced. Once the sauce starts to thicken, remove from the heat and season with salt and pepper.

Blend the sauce in a food processor or with a stick blender until smooth. Set aside in the refrigerator.

Preheat the oven to 180°C (350°F) 15 minutes before serving time. Season the steak with salt and pepper. Heat the remaining oil in a large frying pan over medium–high heat. Add the steak and brown both sides, then place it on an oven tray and cook it in the oven for 5 minutes on each side.

Remove the steak from the oven, wrap it in foil and let the meat rest for 2–3 minutes on each side before carving and serving with the special sauce on the side.

Suggestion
Serve with home-made potato crisps (p. 242) and a green salad.

GRILLED MEATBALL, ZUCCHINI AND ROSEMARY SKEWERS

Serves 4

2 small sprigs rosemary

2 garlic cloves

700 g (1 lb 9 oz) minced (ground) beef

60 g (2¼ oz) fine semolina

1 egg

3 small zucchini (courgettes)

4 tablespoons olive oil

Special equipment
Skewers

Preparation time
45 minutes

Cooking time
20 minutes

If using wooden skewers, soak them in water until ready to use.

Strip the rosemary leaves from the stems and chop coarsely. Crush the garlic.

Put the minced beef, semolina, garlic and egg into a large bowl. Season with salt and pepper, combine well and shape into evenly sized small meatballs.

Cut the zucchini into small chunks. Thread the meatballs and pieces of zucchini alternately onto the skewers.

Preheat a barbecue or the oven grill (broiler) to high. Cook the skewers for 20 minutes, turning them regularly.

Once the meatballs are cooked, arrange the skewers on a large serving plate. Sprinkle with the rosemary, drizzle over the olive oil, season with salt and pepper and serve.

Suggestion
Serve with mashed potatoes with herbs (p. 304).

FLANK STEAK WITH CARAMELISED SHALLOTS

Serves 4

10 French shallots

80 g (2¾ oz) butter

3 tablespoons
sunflower oil

4 flank steaks (bavette),
about 200 g (7 oz) each

Preparation time
15 minutes

Cooking time
25 minutes

Peel and slice the shallots. Melt the butter with 1 tablespoon of the oil in a saucepan over medium heat. Add the shallots, reduce the heat to low and cook for 20 minutes, stirring, until the shallots are very soft but not too brown. Season with salt and pepper. Set aside and keep warm.

Season the steaks with salt and pepper. Heat 2 tablespoons of oil in a large frying pan over high heat. Cook the steaks for 2–3 minutes on each side, until medium-rare or cooked to your taste. Serve on individual plates and top with caramelised shallots.

Suggestion
Serve with crispy potato chips (p. 238).

MEATBALLS IN TOMATO AND CAPSICUM SAUCE

Serves 4

3 red capsicums (peppers)

400 g (14 oz) tinned peeled tomatoes

700 g (1 lb 9 oz) minced (ground) beef

4 sprigs flat-leaf parsley

4 tablespoons olive oil

3 garlic cloves

Special equipment
Food processor

Preparation time
40 minutes

Cooking time
30 minutes

Preheat the oven to 180°C (350°F). Wash and dry the capsicums and bake them whole for 25 minutes. Remove them from the oven, transfer them to a sealed plastic bag and set aside for 5 minutes. Peel the skin off the capsicums using your fingers. Open out the flesh to remove the seeds and cut into pieces.

Put the capsicum pieces and tomatoes with their juice in the bowl of a food processor. Blend until smooth. Set aside.

Wash and chop the parsley leaves. Put the minced meat and parsley into a medium bowl. Season with salt and pepper, knead together with your hands and shape into 12 large balls. Cover and set aside in the refrigerator.

Heat half the olive oil in a flameproof casserole dish over medium–high heat. Add the garlic and meatballs and cook for 5 minutes. Add the tomato and capsicum mixture. Reduce the heat to low and simmer for 30 minutes. Season with salt and pepper, add the remaining olive oil, stir and serve immediately.

ARMENIAN STEAK TARTARE

Serves 4

2 onions

½ bunch flat-leaf parsley

500 g (1 lb 2 oz) freshly minced (ground) beef, put through the mincer (grinder) twice

250 g (9 oz) burghul (bulgur)

Preparation time
20 minutes

Peel and chop the onions. Wash and chop the parsley leaves.

Place the burghul in a bowl of lukewarm water and set aside for 10 minutes, or until the burghul has fully absorbed all of the water and become tender.

Combine the burghul, onion and parsley in a large bowl. Add the minced beef, season with salt and pepper and knead the mixture together using your hand until it is smooth.

Shape the mixture into large oblong meatballs, place them on a large plate and serve immediately.

Suggestion
Serve with potato crisps (p. 242).

SPICY DRY BEEF CURRY

Serves 4

80 g (2¾ oz) butter

3 large red onions

2 garlic cloves

700 g (1 lb 9 oz)
beef tenderloin
(fillet) steak

50 g (1¾ oz) plain
(all-purpose) flour

1 small mild chilli

1 teaspoon ground
coriander

1 teaspoon turmeric

1 teaspoon ground cumin

5 curry leaves

Oil for deep-frying

Plain yoghurt and rice
pancakes, to serve

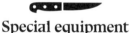

Special equipment
Deep-fryer
(or large saucepan)

Preparation time
20 minutes

Cooking time
15 minutes

To clarify the butter, melt it in a small heavy-based saucepan over medium–high heat, stirring occasionally and removing the froth that forms on the top with a spoon. Let it boil for about 15 minutes, until all the water has evaporated, stirring occasionally. Strain the butter through a fine sieve lined with paper towel into a small glass jar.

Peel and thinly slice the onions and garlic.

Cut the beef into 2.5 cm (1 inch) cubes and toss them in the flour to coat. Heat the clarified butter in a medium saucepan over medium–high heat. Add three-quarters of the onion slices, the garlic and the whole chilli. Cook gently for 4 minutes, then add the coriander, turmeric and cumin. Reduce the heat to medium–low and cook for 5 minutes, stirring. Set aside.

Heat the oil in a deep-fryer or a large saucepan over high heat. The oil is hot enough when a cube of bread turns golden brown in 20 seconds. Add the meat to the hot oil and cook for 3 minutes. Drain and add the meat to the saucepan containing the onions and spices. Mix well, add the curry leaves and return to medium–low heat to cook for 5 minutes, stirring.

Remove from the heat, add the remaining sliced raw onions and season with salt and pepper. Stir through and transfer the curry to a serving plate. Serve immediately with plain yoghurt and rice pancakes.

ROAST BEEF WITH BÉARNAISE SAUCE

Serves 4–6

1 piece roasting beef, about 1 kg (2 lb 4 oz)

2 tablespoons sunflower oil

For the béarnaise sauce

250 g (9 oz) butter

1 large handful tarragon

2 French shallots

50 ml (1½ fl oz) white wine

30 ml (1 fl oz) white vinegar

1 teaspoon freshly ground black pepper

4 egg yolks

Special equipment
Whisk

Preparation time
15 minutes

Cooking time
25 minutes

Meat resting time
10 minutes

To make the béarnaise sauce, first clarify the butter. Melt it in a medium heavy-based saucepan over medium–high heat, stirring occasionally and removing the froth that forms on the top with a spoon. Let it boil for about 15 minutes, until all the water has evaporated, stirring occasionally. Strain the butter through a fine sieve lined with paper towel into a glass jar.

Wash and roughly chop half the tarragon leaves and set them aside. Peel and chop the shallots.

Put the remaining tarragon (with the stems) in a medium saucepan over medium–high heat with the shallots, wine, vinegar and pepper. Bring to the boil, reduce by two-thirds, then set aside to cool.

Preheat the oven to 180°C (350°F).

Add the egg yolks and 5 teaspoons water to the cooled sauce in the saucepan. Place over very low heat and whisk in the yolks vigorously to emulsify the sauce, removing the saucepan from the heat at intervals so the yolks don't curdle. Whisk for 10 minutes, or until the mixture is mousse-like and quite thick.

Remove the saucepan from the heat, add the melted clarified butter and gently whisk it in, as for making mayonnaise. Strain the sauce through a fine strainer and add the reserved chopped tarragon leaves. Put the sauce somewhere that's not too hot or cold.

Season the meat with salt and pepper. Place in a roasting tin and pour the oil over. Cook in the oven for 25 minutes. When cooked, remove from the oven, cover with foil and let the meat rest for 10 minutes, turning it 2–3 times. Cut the roast into slices and serve with the béarnaise sauce on the side.

Suggestion

Serve with fondant potatoes (p. 290) or crispy potato chips (p. 238).

ROAST BEEF CLUB SANDWICHES

Makes 4 sandwiches

20 lettuce leaves of choice

4 tomatoes

2 hard-boiled eggs, peeled

8 thin slices of roast beef

12 slices sandwich bread

4 tablespoons
home-made mayonnaise

Special equipment

Salad spinner

Toothpicks

Preparation time

25 minutes

Wash and spin-dry the lettuce leaves, then remove any tough parts and shred the rest finely. Thinly slice the tomatoes and hard-boiled eggs. Cut the roast beef into thin slices.

Toast the bread. Combine the mayonnaise and lettuce in a bowl.

Lay out 4 slices of toasted bread on a work surface and top with half the dressed lettuce, slices of tomato, roast beef and hard-boiled egg. Place a second slice of toasted bread on top, press down lightly, then add the rest of the lettuce, roast beef, tomato and egg. Top with a final slice of toast and press down lightly.

Before serving, use a large knife to cut each sandwich in half diagonally. Insert a toothpick in the middle of each half to keep the layers together.

BEEF AND WHEAT BERRY STIR-FRY WITH THAI BASIL

Serves 4

700 g (1 lb 9 oz) beef for pan-frying (inside round, rump, tenderloin or striploin)

2 French shallots

4 pink garlic cloves (or white if not available)

1 handful Thai basil

65 ml (2¼ fl oz) olive oil

300 g (10½ oz) cooked wheat berries (or substitute drained tinned corn kernels)

100 ml (3½ fl oz) Japanese-style soy sauce

Preparation time
25 minutes

Cooking time
25 minutes

Slice the beef very thinly and season with salt and pepper. Peel and chop the shallots and garlic. Wash and dry the basil leaves.

Heat the oil in a large frying pan over high heat. Stir-fry the beef for 3 minutes. Transfer to a plate to drain.

Add the shallots and garlic to the pan, reduce the heat to medium and stir-fry for 2–3 minutes, or until beginning to brown. Add the wheatberries, soy sauce, basil leaves and beef, increase the heat to medium–high and stir-fry for 5 minutes, or until all the ingredients are heated through. Serve immediately.

Suggestion
Serve piping hot with steamed Asian vegetables.

GINGER STEAK TARTARE

Serves 4

1 handful chives

5 spring onions (scallions)

100 g (3½ oz) ginger

900 g (2 lb) minced (ground) beef

4 tablespoons soy sauce

100 ml (3½ fl oz) olive oil

Preparation time

15 minutes

Wash and chop the chives. Peel and chop the spring onions, including the green part. Peel and grate the ginger. Set aside these ingredients in the refrigerator. Keep the meat and soy sauce in the refrigerator until ready to serve.

Just before serving time, put the chives, spring onion, the ginger and its juice, the minced beef, olive oil and soy sauce in a large bowl. Add salt, if necessary, and season with pepper, then mix together vigorously with a wooden spatula. Divide the beef between 4 small deep plates or shallow bowls. Serve immediately while still chilled.

Suggestion
Serve chilled with sautéed potatoes with olives and basil (p. 282).

MEXICAN-STYLE GRILLED STEAK WITH PAPRIKA

Serves 6

6 thin steaks (flattened
like escalopes by
your butcher)

2 tablespoons paprika

1 teaspoon chilli powder

115 ml (3¾ fl oz) olive oil

Preparation time
5 minutes

Resting time
Overnight

Cooking time
6 minutes

The day before, put the steak in a shallow dish. In a small bowl, combine the paprika, chilli and olive oil, pour over the steak and cover. Marinate in the refrigerator overnight.

Just before serving time, preheat a barbecue plate or griller (broiler) to high heat. Remove the steaks from the marinade, season with salt and pepper and cook for 3 minutes on each side. Cover the steaks with foil and allow to rest for 3 minutes.

Suggestion
Serve with potato crisps (p. 242) or dauphine potatoes (p. 326).

FAMILY-STYLE BEEF STEW

Serves 4

4 garlic cloves

2 large carrots

1 large onion

2 rashers smoked bacon

40 ml (1¼ fl oz) armagnac (or use cognac or brandy)

1.5 kg (3 lb 5 oz) tri tip steak (bottom sirloin, or use round or rump steak)

200 g (7 oz) pork fat, thinly sliced

4 tablespoons sunflower oil

1 bouquet garni

150 ml (5 fl oz) white wine

1 litre (35 fl oz/4 cups) brown veal stock

500 g (1 lb 2 oz) baby carrots

200 g (7 oz) baby onions

80 g (2¾ oz) butter

50 g (1¾ oz) caster (superfine) sugar

Preparation time
1 hour

Cooking time
2 hours 30 minutes

Bruise the garlic cloves in their skin. Peel the large carrots and slice into rounds. Peel and chop the large onion. Finely chop the bacon and soak it in the armagnac. Roll the pork fat around the beef.

Preheat the oven to 170°C (325°F).

Heat 2 tablespoons of the oil in a large flameproof casserole dish over high heat. Brown the beef on all sides and transfer to a plate. Add the garlic, carrot rounds, onion and bouquet garni to the casserole dish. Cook for 5 minutes. Pour in the wine and boil, stirring, for 30 seconds to deglaze the pan. Strain and reserve the bacon, adding the armagnac to the pan with the stock. Return the beef to the casserole dish, cover with a lid and cook in the oven for 2½ hours.

Meanwhile, peel the baby carrots and onions. Heat the remaining 2 tablespoons of oil and the butter in a frying pan over medium heat. Add the carrots and onions and sweat them for 3 minutes without browning. Add the caster sugar and add water to almost cover. Cook until the liquid has evaporated, then reduce the heat to low and add the reserved bacon pieces from the armagnac. Cook gently for 10–15 minutes, stirring occasionally. Season with salt and pepper.

Remove the casserole dish from the oven and transfer the beef to a serving dish. Add the carrots, onions and bacon from the frying pan Strain the sauce and pour it over the meat. Adjust the seasoning if necessary and serve immediately.

MEATBALLS IN SAFFRON BROTH

Serves 4–6

2 garlic cloves

2 sage leaves

4 tablespoons olive oil

1 sprig thyme

1 teaspoon tomato paste (concentrated purée)

250 ml (9 fl oz/1 cup) white wine

250 ml (9 fl oz/1 cup) beef stock

10 saffron threads

700 g (1 lb 9 oz) minced (ground) beef

100 g (3½ oz) almond meal

2 eggs

Preparation time

35 minutes

Cooking time

35 minutes

Peel and chop the garlic cloves. Wash and chop the sage. Heat the olive oil in a large saucepan over medium heat. Add the garlic, sage, thyme and tomato paste and cook gently for 2 minutes, stirring. Add the wine and cook until reduced by one-quarter. Reduce the heat to low, add the stock and saffron and simmer gently for 2 minutes. Set aside.

Combine the minced beef, almond meal and eggs in a large bowl. Season with salt and pepper and shape into meatballs the size of an egg. Return the saucepan to the stovetop over low heat and add the meatballs to the broth. Cook for 25 minutes, season and serve.

Suggestion

Serve these meatballs and their broth with steamed potatoes.

BEEF, PEAR AND CHEESE TURNOVERS

Serves 4–6

2 sheets (25 x 50 cm/
10 x 20 inches) frozen
puff pastry, thawed

2 cooking pears

300 g (10½) washed
rind cheese (such as
Taleggio, Epoisses or
Pont-l'Evêque)

500 g (1 lb 2 oz) minced
(ground) beef

2 egg yolks

Preparation time
35 minutes

Cooking time
35 minutes

Preheat the oven to 180°C (350°F).

Cut out 4 puff pastry circles of 18 cm (17 inch) diameter.

Peel, core and finely dice the pears. Remove the rind from the cheese and cut the cheese into small pieces.

Combine the pear, cheese and minced beef in a mixing bowl. Season with salt and pepper.

Divide the mixture between the 4 pastry circles, placing it in the centre. Brush the edges with a little water and fold them in towards the middle, pressing the edges together to seal the pastry. Place the turnovers on a baking tray lined with baking paper. Whisk the egg yolks with a little cold water and brush over the pastry. Bake for 35 minutes, or until cooked through and golden brown.

Suggestion

Serve these turnovers hot with a green salad.

BEEF RIBS IN CAPSICUM BARBECUE SAUCE

Serves 4

1.2 kg (2 lb 7 oz) beef short ribs (ask the butcher to cut them into pieces)

For the sauce

1 onion

3 garlic cloves

2 red capsicums (peppers)

3 tablespoons olive oil

2 tablespoons tomato sauce (ketchup)

4 tablespoons honey

100 g (3½ oz) tomato paste (concentrated purée)

2 tablespoons soy sauce

100 ml (3½ fl oz) red wine

2 tablespoons mustard

4 sprigs thyme

Special equipment
Stick (hand) blender

Preparation time
25 minutes

Cooking time
2 hours 15 minutes

Put the ribs in a large saucepan with 2 litres (70 fl oz/8 cups) water over medium–high heat. Bring to the boil, reduce the heat to low and cook for 2 hours. Drain and set aside.

Meanwhile, to make the barbecue sauce, peel and chop the onion and garlic. De-stem and seed the capsicums, then cut the flesh into small pieces. Heat the olive oil in a medium saucepan over medium heat. Add the onion and garlic and cook for 1–2 minutes, stirring. Add the capsicum, tomato sauce, honey, tomato paste, 50 ml cooking liquid from the ribs, the soy sauce, wine and mustard and stir to combine. Reduce the heat to very low and cook for 45 minutes, stirring occasionally.

Preheat the oven to 180°C (350°F). Purée the sauce with a stick (hand) blender. Season with salt and pepper. Arrange the ribs in a large heatproof dish, pour the barbecue sauce over and bake for 15 minutes, or until the ribs are slightly glazed.

Garnish with thyme sprigs and serve.

Suggestion
Serve immediately with potato crisps (p. 242).

BRAISED RIB STEAK

Serves 4

4 garlic cloves

1 thick rib steak
(about 1.4 kg/3 lb 2 oz)

4 tablespoons
sunflower oil

50 g (1¾ oz) butter

2 bay leaves

Preparation time
15 minutes

Cooking time
20 minutes

Meat resting time
10 minutes

Bruise the garlic cloves in their skin. Season the rib steak with salt and pepper. Heat the oil and butter in a cast-iron flameproof casserole dish over high heat. Add the steak, garlic cloves and bay leaves and cook for 5 minutes. Carefully turn the rib steak over, reduce the heat to medium–low and cook for another 10 minutes, basting regularly with the cooking juices.

Transfer the steak to a plate, cover with foil and let it rest for 10 minutes. Cut the steak into thick slices and drizzle with the cooking juices.

Suggestion

Serve immediately with soufflé potatoes (p. 250) or crispy potato chips (p. 238).

HAMBURGERS WITH GRILLED CAPSICUM

Makes 4 hamburgers

2 red capsicums (peppers)

700 g (1 lb 9 oz) minced (ground) beef

1 tablespoon sunflower oil

4 tablespoons olive oil

8 bacon rashers (optional)

4 round hamburger or brioche buns

4 thick slices cheddar cheese (optional)

4 lettuce leaves

For the sauce
1 tablespoon dijon mustard

2 tablespoons tomato sauce (ketchup)

4 tablespoons mayonnaise

5–8 drops Tabasco sauce

Preparation time
35 minutes

Cooking time
35 minutes

Preheat the oven to 180°C (350°F).

Wash the capsicums and place them whole on an oven tray. Cook in the oven for 25 minutes. Remove the capsicums and reduce the heat to 170°C (325°F).

Cool the capsicums in a plastic bag for 5 minutes, then peel off the skin. Pull open the capsicums and remove the seeds. Cut the flesh into pieces. Set aside.

Season the minced beef with salt and pepper. Use your hands to shape the mince into 4 quite thick round patties.

Heat the sunflower and olive oils in a large frying pan over medium–high heat. Add the bacon and cook until crispy. Transfer to paper towel on a plate to drain.

Add the meat patties to the pan and cook for 4–8 minutes each side, or until cooked to your liking, basting them with the pan juices. Set aside and keep warm.

To make the sauce, mix together the mustard, tomato sauce, mayonnaise and Tabasco.

Cut the buns in half. Spread sauce over the bottom halves and put on an oven tray or in a large ovenproof dish. Put the cooked meat patties on top of the sauce, and top with a slice of cheese, if using. Put the tray in the oven for 3 minutes to melt the cheese.

Add the bacon, capsicum, lettuce and the top half of the buns.

Suggestion
Serve with gherkins (pickles) and crispy potato chips (p. 238).

MARINATED BEEF SKEWERS SPRINKLED WITH DRIED HERBS

Serves 6

1 kg (2 lb 4 oz) tender
beef, such as sirloin
or rump steak, cut into
2.5 cm (1 inch) cubes

1 teaspoon curry powder

50 ml (1½ fl oz) olive oil

3 large red onions

1 large green
capsicum (pepper)

1 large red
capsicum (pepper)

1 large yellow
capsicum (pepper)

1 teaspoon dried oregano

1 teaspoon dried thyme

1 teaspoon dried mint

Special equipment
Skewers

Preparation time
45 minutes

Resting time
Overnight

Cooking time
20 minutes

The day before, place the meat in a large bowl with the curry powder and oil, and season with salt and pepper. Combine well, cover with plastic wrap and marinate overnight in the refrigerator.

On serving day, if using wooden skewers, soak them in water until ready to use. Peel the onions and cut them lengthways into four pieces. De-stem and seed the capsicums, and cut them into small pieces. Cut up the onions in the same way and separate the layers of onion with your fingers to obtain evenly sized pieces.

Preheat the barbecue to medium–high. Thread the marinated beef pieces onto the skewers, with slices of onion and capsicum in between. Combine the dried herbs, sprinkle over the skewers and season with salt and pepper. Cook the skewers on the barbecue until rare, or cooked to your liking.

Suggestion
Serve with barbecued potatoes with rosemary oil (p. 300).

GRILLED STEAK WITH HERB AND WATERCRESS SAUCE

Serves 4–5

1 kg (2 lb 4 oz) topside steak

For the sauce

1 small handful watercress

1 handful tarragon

10 sprigs basil

2 garlic cloves

100 ml (3½ fl oz) olive oil

1 teaspoon dried thyme

Preparation time
20 minutes

Cooking time
4–8 minutes

Meat resting time
2–4 minutes

To make the sauce, wash, pick and roughly chop the watercress leaves. Wash the tarragon and basil and pick the leaves. Peel and chop the garlic.

Heat the oil in a small saucepan over medium–high heat. Add the garlic and thyme and cook them for 20 seconds, stirring. Remove from the heat. Transfer to a bowl and set aside to cool until just warm. Add the watercress, tarragon and basil, season with salt and pepper and set aside.

Cut the meat into several thick slices. Heat a barbecue rack or a frying pan over high heat.

Five minutes before serving time, season the meat with salt and pepper and place on the hot barbecue or in the hot frying pan. Cook the meat for 2 minutes on each side for rare, or 4 minutes for medium-rare.

Transfer the meat to a plate, cover with foil and let it rest in a warm place for half the cooking time, turning over at least once to distribute the juices in the meat. Serve with the herb and watercress sauce.

Suggestion

Serve this steak with crispy potato chips (p. 238).

BELGIAN BEEF AND BEER STEW

Serves 4–6

1.2 kg (2 lb 11 oz) stewing beef, such as blade, chuck or shin

2 rashers bacon or 2 slices speck

2 large onions

2 tablespoons sunflower oil

2 tablespoons raw (demerara) sugar

1 litre (35 fl oz/4 cups) stout-style beer

2 slices pain d'épice (spiced sweet French quick bread)

2 bay leaves

1 sprig thyme

Preparation time

25 minutes

Cooking time

2 hours

Cut the meat into large cubes and the smoked bacon into large chunks. Peel the onions and chop them roughly.

Heat the oil in a flameproof casserole dish over medium–high heat. Add the meat and brown on all sides. Transfer to a plate.

Increase the heat to high, add the onions and raw sugar to the cooking juices and cook for 5 minutes, stirring. Pour in the beer, and boil, stirring, for 30 seconds to deglaze the pan. Return the meat to the dish and add the pain d'épices, broken into pieces. Reduce the heat to low, add the bay leaves and thyme, and simmer for 2 hours, or until cooked and tender, stirring occasionally. Season to taste with salt and pepper.

Suggestion

Serve hot with crispy potato chips (p. 238).

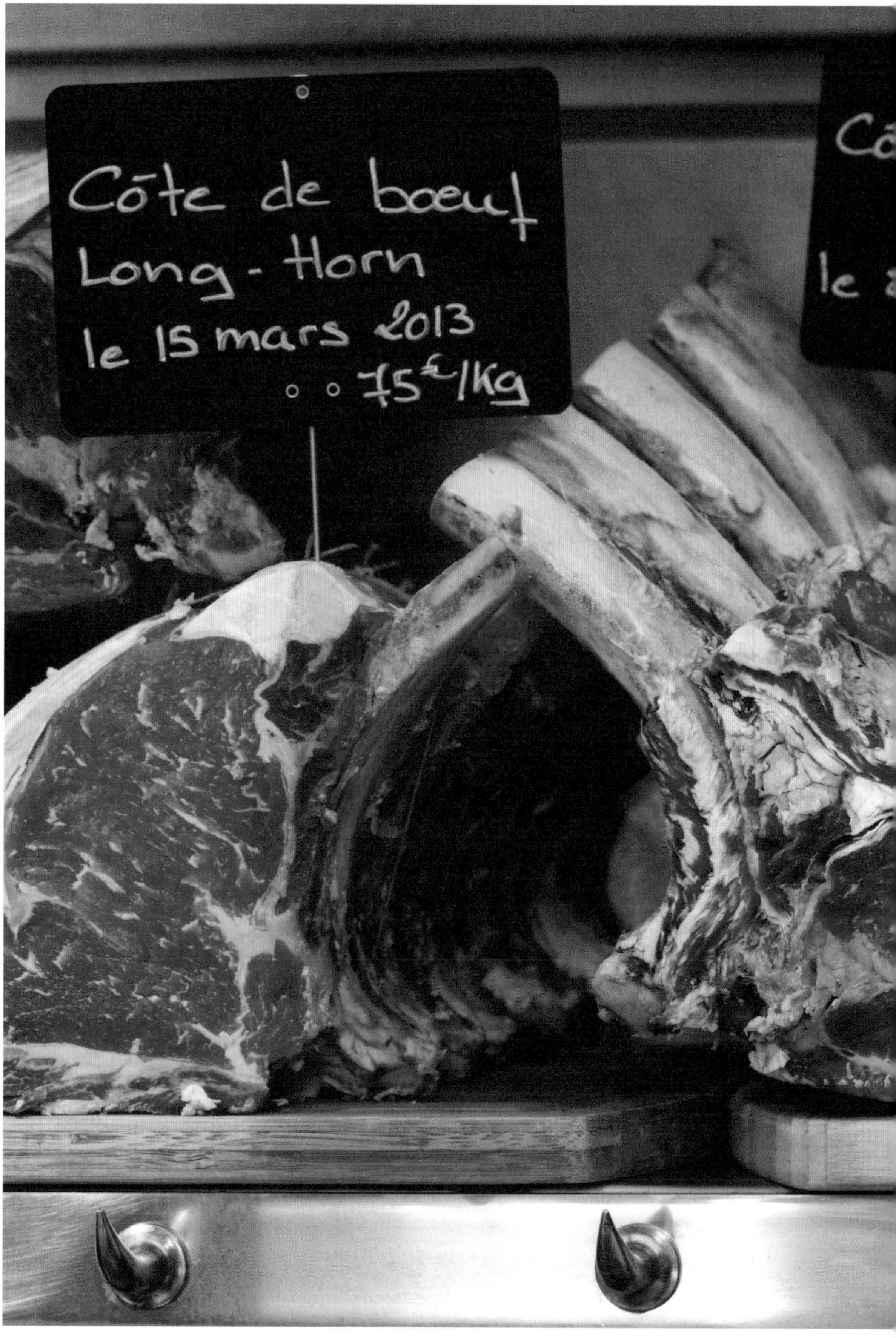

Côte de bœuf
Long - Horn
le 15 mars 2013
○ ○ 75€/kg

de boeuf
ngus
mars 2013
75€/kg
Côte de boeuf
Long-Horn
le 8 mars 2013
75€/kg

BEEF AND CHEESE CROQUETTES

Serves 4

250 g (9 oz) mimolette, parmesan or aged cheddar cheese

2 garlic cloves

500 g (1 lb 2 oz) minced (ground) beef

2 eggs

10 tablespoons toasted breadcrumbs

Oil for deep frying

Special equipment
Cheese grater

Preparation time
25 minutes

Cooking time
5 minutes

Grate the cheese. Peel and chop the garlic cloves.

Combine the minced beef, garlic and cheese in a bowl. Shape the mixture into small oval-shaped meatballs with your fingers.

Beat the eggs in a small bowl. Put the breadcrumbs in a shallow bowl. Dip the meatballs in the beaten egg, then in the breadcrumbs.

Heat the oil in a deep-fryer or a medium saucepan over high heat until it reaches 180°C (350°F), or when a cube of bread turns golden in 15 seconds. Deep-fry the meatballs for 1–2 minutes, until they are brown and cooked through. Drain the meatballs on paper towel and let them cool for 1–2 minutes before serving.

Suggestion
Serve with a green salad and crispy potato chips (p. 238).

HANGER STEAK AND APRICOT SKEWERS WITH CUMIN

Serves 4

600 g (1 lb 5 oz) hanger (thick skirt) steak

12 dried apricots

1 tablespoon ground cumin

4 tablespoons soy sauce

2 tablespoons olive oil, plus 1 tablespoon extra for frying (optional)

A few radicchio leaves

Special equipment
Small skewers

Preparation time
35 minutes

Resting time
2 hours

Cooking time
10 minutes

If using wooden skewers, soak them in water until ready to use.

Cut the meat and apricots into 2.5 cm (1 inch) cubes. Assemble small skewers, alternating the cubes of steak and pieces of apricot. Place the skewers in a large flat dish, and sprinkle over the cumin, olive oil and soy sauce. Cover with plastic wrap and marinate for 2 hours in the refrigerator.

When ready to cook, preheat the barbecue or heat the extra oil in a large frying pan over medium–high heat. Cook the skewers for 2–3 minutes on each side. Serve the grilled skewerss on a bed of radicchio leaves.

Suggestion

Serve hot with baked jacket potatoes or new potatoes in their skin with sage butter (p. 240).

BEEF AND CHILLI EMPANADAS

Serves 4

For the pastry

250 g cornflour
(cornstarch)

100 ml (3½ fl oz) olive oil

1 pinch salt

For the filling

2 small tomatoes

2 garlic cloves

2 large onions

4 tablespoons olive oil

500 g (1 lb 2 oz) minced
(ground) beef

1 tablespoon paprika

Preparation time
45 minutes

Resting time
45 minutes

Cooking time
45 minutes

To make the pastry, mix the cornflour, oil and 250 ml (9 fl oz/1 cup) water together in a bowl with your fingertips until a ball of dough comes together. Wrap the dough in plastic wrap and let it rest in the refrigerator for 45 minutes.

To make the filling, meanwhile, de-stem and seed the tomatoes and cut them into small dice. Peel and chop the garlic and onions. Heat the olive oil in a large frying pan over medium–low heat. Add the onion and garlic and cook gently, stirring, for 2–3 minutes. Add the minced beef, paprika and tomato. Cook, stirring, until the mixture is dry.

Preheat the oven to 180°C (350°F). Line a baking tray with a sheet of baking paper.

Roll out the dough on a work surface to 5 mm (¼ inch) thick. Cut out 4 circles of dough, top each with a quarter of the filling and fold over to form semi-circles. Press the edges together to seal the pastry and make small turnovers.

Put the dough parcels on the lined baking tray and cook in the preheated oven for 30 minutes. Serve the empanadas warm.

BEEF MEATBALLS WITH SILVERBEET AND HERBS

Serves 8

4 French shallots

2 rashers bacon or
2 slices speck

1 kg (2 lb 4 oz) silverbeet
(Swiss chard)

1.4 kg (3 lb 2 oz) minced
(ground) beef

1 tablespoon herbs
de Provence or mixed
dried herbs

5 sprigs flat-leaf parsley

500 g (1 lb 2 oz) pork
caul fat

Special equipment

Food processor

Preparation time

45 minutes

Cooking time

1 hour 30 minutes

Peel and chop the shallots. Cut the bacon into small pieces.

Wash and trim the silverbeet, then chop coarsely. Put the silverbeet into a large saucepan, cover with boiling water and cook over for medium heat for 30 minutes. Drain well.

Preheat the oven to 180°C (350°C).

Process the shallots, bacon and cooked silverbeet in a food processor. Add the minced beef, herbs de Provence and parsley, season with salt and pepper and process until smooth.

Shape the mince mixture into large balls, about 180 g (6½ oz) each. Wrap the meatballs in the caul fat and place them in a large baking dish. Cook in the preheated oven for 1½ hours, basting the meatballs (known as 'caillettes') with the cooking juices at intervals, or until cooked through and golden. Serve hot.

Suggestion

Serve with sautéed potatoes with olives and basil (p. 282).

PROVENÇAL BEEF STEW

Serves 4–6 • 1.5 kg (3 lb 5 oz) stewing beef, such as blade, chuck or shin \ 1 large onion \ 2 carrots\ 4 garlic cloves \ 2 rashers bacon, rind removed, or 2 slices speck \ 4 tablespoons olive oil \ 2 sprigs thyme \ 1 bay leaf \ 1 tablespoon plain (all-purpose) flour \ 1 bottle (750 ml/26 fl oz/3 cups) Côtes de Provence or rosé wine \ Zest of 1 orange or mandarin

Special equipment • Cast-iron casserole dish (with lid) \ Zester

Preparation time • 30 minutes

Cooking time • 3 hours 10 minutes

Cut the meat into large cubes. Peel and chop the onion. Peel the carrots and cut them in two lengthways. Bruise the garlic cloves in their skin. Cut the bacon into large chunks.

Heat the olive oil in a large cast-iron flameproof casserole dish over medium–high heat and brown the beef on all sides. Add the onion, bacon, garlic, thyme and bay leaf. Cook for 2–3 minutes, then add the flour, mixing it through with a spatula. Season with salt and pepper. Reduce the heat to medium–low.

Blend in the red wine and add the orange zest, carrots and 200 ml (7 fl oz) water. Reduce the heat to low and simmer, covered, for 3 hours, stirring occasionally.

When the stew (also called a 'daube', after the pot it was originally cooked in) is cooked and meltingly tender, adjust the seasoning. Serve with polenta, potato purée with olive oil (p. 294) or chickpea chips (see below).

CHICKPEA CHIPS

Serves 6 • 250 g (9 oz) chickpea flour (besan) \ ½ teaspoon ground cumin \ a little olive oil for greasing \ olive oil for deep-frying

Special equipment • Deep-fryer (or large saucepan)

Preparation time • 15 minutes

Cooking time • 10 minutes

Resting time • Overnight

The day before, bring 1 litre (35 fl oz/4 cups) water to a simmer in a large saucepan over medium heat and add the chickpea flour in a stream, stirring gently with a spatula. Once the mixture thickens, remove from the heat, season with salt and pepper and continue stirring for 1 minute.

Pour this mixture into an oiled dish, spread it out evenly, then cover with plastic wrap and let it set overnight in the refrigerator.

The next day, cut the set mixture into large evenly sized chips (also called 'panisses'). Heat the olive oil in a deep-fryer or a large saucepan over high heat to 160°C (315°F), or when a cube of bread turns golden brown in 30–35 seconds. Cook the chips for 1–2 minutes, drain and season with salt.

ROLLED STEAK AND CHEESE

Serves 4

2 large onions

50 g (1¾ oz) butter

2 tablespoons sunflower oil

4 very thin flank (bavette) steaks, about 170 g (5¾ oz) each

1 teaspoon dijon mustard

200 g (7 oz) comté (or strong gruyère) cheese

8 sprigs tarragon

1 bay leaf

Special equipment

A sharp knife

Preparation time

20 minutes

Cooking time

40 minutes

Peel and thinly slice the onions. Heat the butter and 1 tablespoon of the oil in a large saucepan over medium–low heat. Add the onions and sauté them gently over low heat for 30 minutes, stirring regularly, until they have browned and softened.

Cut the steaks in half and spread with mustard. Place a thick slice of cheese and a sprig of tarragon in the middle of each slice, and roll up. Arrange the rolls in a baking dish (placing the join of the rolls downwards) with the bay leaf. Season with salt and pepper and sprinkle over the remaining oil.

Preheat the oven grill (broiler) to medium–high and cook the rolled steak and cheese for 10 minutes (the cheese should melt slightly). Serve the rolls with the onions, and mashed potato with a knob of butter.

CHILLI BEEF AND CAPSICUM FAJITAS

Serves 4

1 onion

2 yellow capsicums (peppers)

4 tablespoons olive oil

1 teaspoon chilli powder

4 sprigs thyme, plus extra, to serve

50 ml (1½ fl oz) tomato passata (puréed tomatoes)

700 g (1 lb 9 oz) minced (ground) beef

12 small tortillas

Lettuce leaves, to serve

Preparation time
25 minutes

Cooking time
15 minutes

Peel and chop the onion. De-stem, seed and slice the capsicums. Heat the oil in a frying pan over medium–high heat. Add the capsicums and onion and cook for 10 minutes. Add the chilli, thyme, tomato passata and minced beef. Reduce the heat to low, season with salt and pepper and simmer for 5 minutes. Remove from the heat.

Serve with lettuce leaves, salad vegetables and the tortillas, warmed for a few moments in the microwave oven. Top with the extra thyme.

Suggestion

You can increase the amount of chilli for more spice.

SAUTÉED BEEF WITH MINTED PEAS

Serves 4

2 garlic cloves

1 red onion

15 fresh mint leaves

700 g (1 lb 9 oz) beef
for pan-frying (topside,
rump, tenderloin or
striploin)

4 tablespoons olive oil

250 g (9 oz) fresh or
frozen peas

4 tablespoons soy sauce

Preparation time
25 minutes

Cooking time
10–12 minutes

Peel and chop the garlic and onion. Wash and chop the mint. Cut the meat into small, thin slices.

Heat 2 tablespoons of the oil in a large frying pan over medium–high heat. Add the onions and cook quickly. Add the peas, season with salt and pepper and sauté for 4 minutes, stirring. Set aside on a plate.

Wipe out the frying pan and heat the remaining oil over medium–high heat. Add the meat and cook for 2–3 minutes, tossing frequently.

Add the soy sauce and boil, stirring, for 30 seconds to deglaze the pan. Cook until the liquid is reduced by half, then add the mint and peas. Increase the heat to high and cook for 2 minutes. Remove from the heat and serve hot.

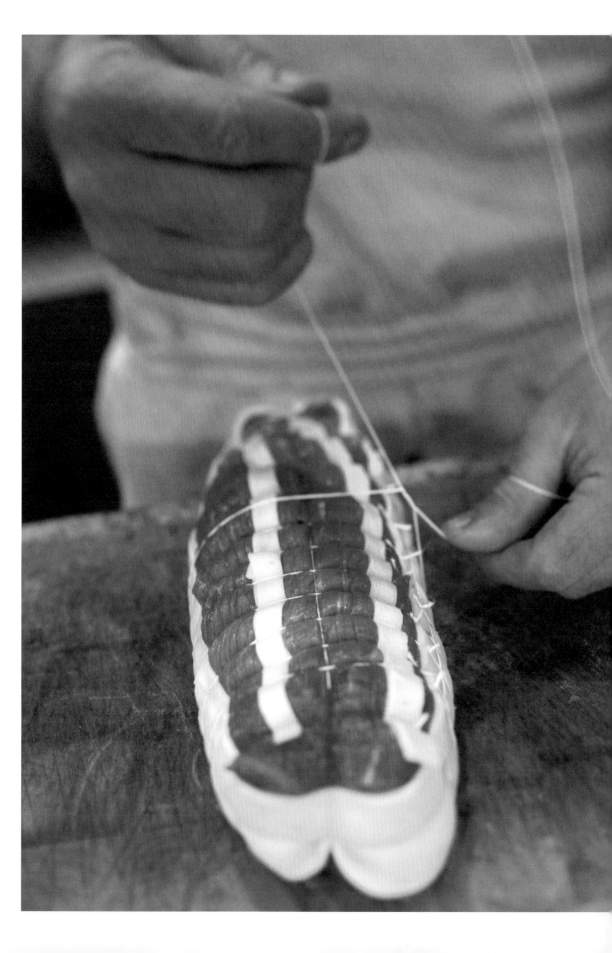

POACHED BEEF WITH VEGETABLES

Serves 4

1 kg (2 lb 4 oz) beef
tenderloin, topside,
bottom sirloin (tri-tip)
or rump, rolled and tied
into a roast

For the stock

4 carrots

4 turnips

2 leeks

1 celery stalk

500 g (1 lb 2 oz) oxtail

1 bouquet garni

Special equipment

Fine strainer (chinois)

Stockpot and cast-iron
casserole dish

Preparation time

25 minutes

Cooking time

2 hours (stock)
20 minutes (beef)

To make the stock, peel the carrots and turnips. Wash the leeks and tie them together. Wash and dry the celery.

Place the oxtail in a stockpot and add water to just reach the top of the meat. Place over high heat and bring to the boil. Reduce to medium–low heat and simmer for 5 minutes. Drain the oxtail, discard the water and wash the stockpot.

Return the oxtail to the stockpot and add the carrots, turnips, leeks, celery and bouquet garni. Add water just to the top of the oxtail and vegetables and cook for 2 hours over low heat. Remove the vegetables, cut them into small pieces and set them aside in a warm place. Strain the remaining stock using a fine strainer (chinois) and adjust the seasoning. Reserve the oxtail for another use, if desired.

Thirty minutes before serving time, bring the stock to the boil in a cast-iron casserole dish. Add the rolled beef, reduce the heat to low and poach for 20 minutes. Remove the meat and cut into thick slices.

Serve the poached beef with the vegetables, steamed potatoes and a bowl of the poaching liquid.

Tip

To save time, you can make the stock the day before.

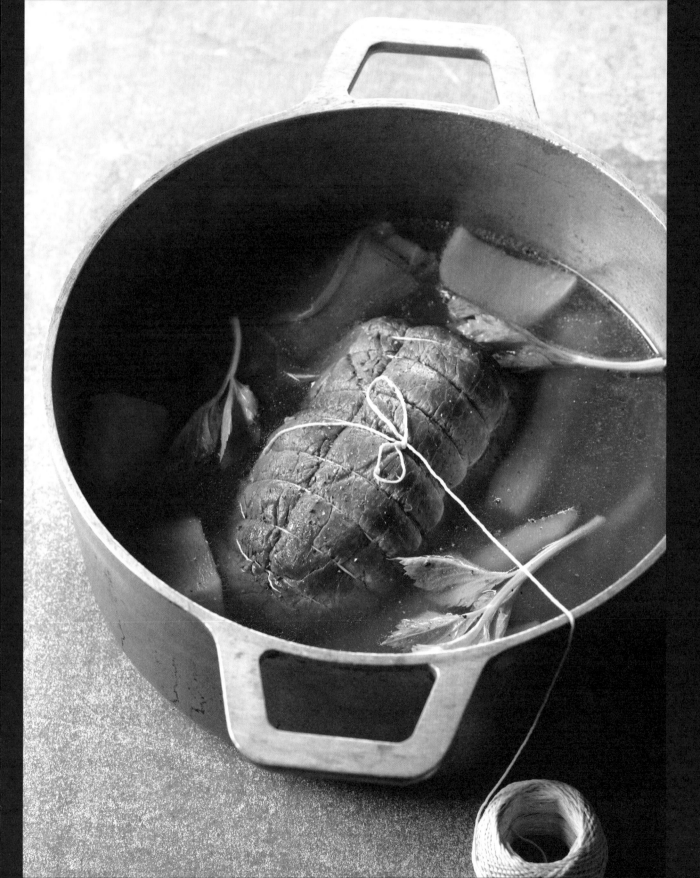

BEEF STIR-FRY WITH THAI BASIL

Serves 4–6

700 g (1 lb 9 oz) beef
for pan-frying (topside,
rump, tenderloin
or striploin)

100 g (3½ oz) ginger

3 garlic cloves

3 tablespoons olive oil,
plus 1 teaspoon extra

1 handful Thai basil

80 g (2¾ oz)
salted peanuts

1 pinch chilli powder

Special equipment
Grater

Garlic crusher

Mortar and pestle

Preparation time
10 minutes

Cooking time
5 minutes

Slice the beef very thinly. Peel and grate the ginger. Peel and crush the garlic. Place the beef, ginger, garlic and the 3 tablespoons of olive oil in a large bowl. Mix, cover with plastic wrap and leave to marinate for 30 minutes at room temperature.

Meanwhile, pick the leaves from the basil, wash them and set aside. Heat the extra 1 teaspoon olive oil in a frying pan over medium heat. Add the peanuts and cook until lightly browned. Drain them on paper towel and crush them roughly in a mortar or using a rolling pin.

Heat a large frying pan over high heat. Add the beef and marinade and stir-fry for 2–3 minutes. Add the chilli powder and stir-fry for a further 1 minute. Add the Thai basil, toss through and remove the pan from the heat.

Serve the stir-fry very hot in individual bowls with the peanuts scattered over the top.

BRAISED BEEF
WITH MADEIRA

Serves 4–6

3 tablespoons
sunflower oil, plus
2 tablespoons extra

1.5 kg (3 lb 5 oz) stewing
beef (blade, chuck or
shin), cut into large cubes

1 large sprig thyme

2 bay leaves

250 ml (9 fl oz/1 cup)
madeira (or dry muscat)

250 ml (9 fl oz/1 cup)
brown veal stock

250 g (9 oz) baby onions

250 g (9 oz) small
mushrooms

80 g (2¾ oz) butter

1 teaspoon caster
(superfine) sugar

250 g (9 oz) diced bacon
or speck

Special equipment
Cast-iron casserole dish

Preparation time
35 minutes

Cooking time
2 hours 10 minutes

Heat the 3 tablespoons of oil in a large cast-iron casserole dish over high heat. Add the beef cubes and cook until browned on all sides. Add the thyme and bay leaves and cook, stirring, for 5 minutes.

Add the madeira and let it reduce. Add the stock and season with salt and pepper. Reduce the heat to low, cover and simmer for 2 hours.

Meanwhile, peel the baby onions. De-stem, wash and dry the mushrooms. Heat 1 tablespoon of the extra oil in a frying pan over high heat. Add the mushrooms and cook for 1–2 minutes, or until browned. Set aside.

Put 50 g (1¾ oz) of the butter and the remaining 1 tablespoon of oil in a large, deep frying pan over medium–high heat. Add the onions and cook for 2–3 minutes, or until browned. Add the sugar and cook, stirring, until caramelised. Pour in 50 ml (1½ fl oz) water and boil, stirring, for 30 seconds to deglaze the pan. Reduce the heat to medium–low, add the bacon and cook gently for 10–15 minutes, stirring occasionally. Add the mushrooms and the remaining butter. Season with salt and pepper.

At serving time, add the caramelised onion and mushroom mixture to the casserole. Bring to the boil, adjust the seasoning and place the casserole dish on the table and serve.

BEEF AND CHEESE SKEWERS WITH CURRY CRUMBS

Serves 4

700 g (1 lb 9 oz) beef
for pan-frying (topside,
rump, tenderloin
or striploin)

200 g (7 oz) comté cheese
(or gruyère or aged
cheddar)

2 teaspoons curry powder

2 tablespoons
breadcrumbs

2 tablespoons olive oil

Special equipment
Skewers

Preparation time
25 minutes

Cooking time
15 minutes

If using wooden skewers, soak them in water until ready to use.

Cut the meat and cheese into cubes of the same size, about 2.5 cm (1 inch), then assemble the skewers, alternating a cube of meat and a cube of cheese.

Combine the curry powder with the breadcrumbs.

Preheat a barbecue to medium-high or place a large frying pan over medium–high heat. Season the skewered meat and cheese with salt and pepper, coat with the curry breadcrumbs and brush with the olive oil. Cook the skewers on the barbecue or in the frying pan for 2–3 minutes, or until the meat is cooked to your liking but the cheese hasn't melted too much.

Suggestion
Serve hot with a green salad and potatoes baked in coals.

ROQUEFORT STEAK

Serves 4

200 g (7 oz) roquefort cheese

4 sprigs flat-leaf parsley

1 small handful chives

10 walnuts, shelled

4 rump or tenderloin steaks (about 200 g/7 oz each)

2 tablespoons sunflower oil

50 g (1¾ oz) butter

Rocket (arugula), to serve

Preparation time
5 minutes

Cooking time
10 minutes

Cut the roquefort into four pieces. Wash and chop the parsley leaves. Wash and chop the chives. Roughly chop the walnuts.

Season the steaks with salt and pepper. Heat the oil in a frying pan over medium–high heat and add the steaks. Add the butter and cook the steaks for 4–5 minutes on each side, basting regularly with the cooking juices.

Arrange the rocket on 4 individual plates. Put the steaks on the rocket and place a piece of roquefort on each. Sprinkle with the chopped walnuts, parsley and chives, spoon over a little of the hot cooking juices and serve immediately.

Suggestion
Enjoy these roquefort steaks dressed with a little walnut oil.

POT-AU-FEU TERRINE WITH TARRAGON

Serves 6

1 handful tarragon

100 g (3½ oz) cornichons (small gherkins/pickles)

9 sheets (20 g) gelatine

800 g (1 lb 12 oz) cooked beef, such as leftover pot-au-feu

100 g (3½ oz) capers, rinsed

1 litre (35 fl oz/4 cups) beef broth from a pot-au-feu, all fat skimmed off

Special equipment
Whisk

Terrine dish

Preparation time
15 minutes

Cooking time
10 minutes

Resting time
12 hours

Wash and chop the tarragon leaves. Roughly chop the cornichons. Put the gelatine sheets in a bowl of cold water to soften. Shred the meat and mix in a bowl with the tarragon, cornichons and capers.

Bring the broth to the boil over high heat then remove from the heat. Drain and squeeze out the sheets of gelatine, add them to the hot broth and whisk until dissolved. Add the broth to the meat mixture in the bowl and season with salt and pepper. Stir to combine then pour the mixture into a terrine dish.

Let the terrine set in the refrigerator for 12 hours.

Unmould the terrine onto a board and cut into thick slices to serve with toast.

BEEF SASHIMI

Serves 4

2 carrots

150 g (5½ oz) daikon
(white radish)

8 shiso leaves

4 small (150 g/5½ oz)
wagyu steaks

Shredded raw vegetables,
to serve

40 g (1½ oz) wasabi,
powdered or from a tube

160 ml (5¼ fl oz)
soy sauce

Special equipment
Food processor

Preparation time
20 minutes

Cooking time
2 minutes

Peel the carrots and daikon, then grate in a food processor on a medium blade. Wash and finely shred half the shiso leaves (set the remainder aside). Combine the daikon, carrots and shredded shiso in a mixing bowl. Season with salt and pepper.

Heat a large dry non-stick frying pan over high heat (do not add any oil). Cook the steaks for 1 minute (a dry crust will form). Season with salt and pepper, turn the steaks over and cook for 1 minute. Season the steaks with salt and pepper again, remove from the heat and set aside to cool.

Cut the the cooled steaks into thin, even slices. Arrange the beef sashimi on small plates on a bed of grated vegetables. Add a little wasabi. Garnish with the whole shiso leaves and serve with the soy sauce and wasabi.

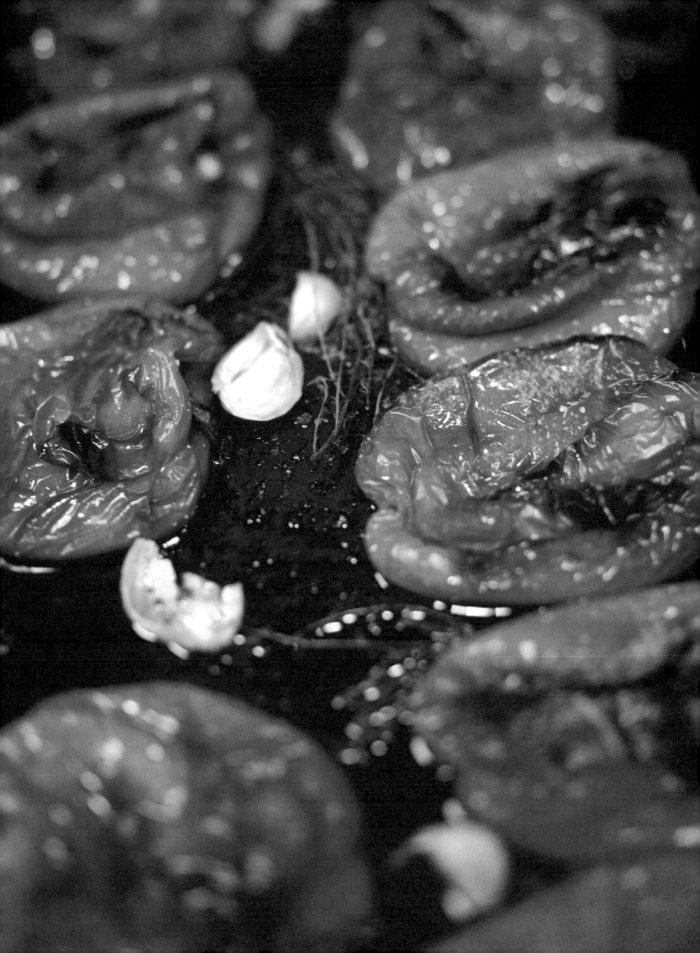

BRAISED OXTAIL WITH TOMATO AND CITRUS

Serves 4–6

2 organic lemons

2 organic oranges

1 organic grapefruit

2 large onions

4 garlic cloves

80 g (2¾ oz) butter

4 tablespoons olive oil

1.5 kg oxtail (3 lb 5 oz), cut into thick slices

2 bay leaves

1 sprig thyme

500 ml (17 fl oz/2 cups) white wine

1.6 kg (1 lb 12 oz) tinned peeled tomatoes

Special equipment

Zester

Citrus juicer

Cast-iron casserole dish

Preparation time

35 minutes

Cooking time

2 hours 15 minutes

Zest all of the citrus fruit and juice the lemons. Set aside. Peel and slice the onions. Bruise the garlic cloves in their skin.

Heat the butter and olive oil in a large cast-iron casserole dish over medium–high heat. Add the oxtail, onion, garlic, bay leaves and thyme and cook for 2–3 minutes, stirring. Season with salt and pepper and add the white wine. Cook until the liquid is reduced by a quarter. Add the tomatoes with their juice, the citrus zest and lemon juice. Reduce the heat to low and gently simmer for 2 hours.

Test the meat with a knife to ensure it is cooked through and very tender, and adjust the seasoning.

SKIRT STEAK WITH MUSTARD CREAM

Serves 4

2 French shallots

60 g (2¼ oz) butter

50 ml (1½ fl oz)
white wine

250 ml (9 fl oz/1 cup)
thin (pouring) cream

1 tablespoon
strong mustard

2 tablespoons
wholegrain mustard

2 tablespoons
sunflower oil

800 g (1 lb 12 oz) thin
(outside) skirt steak,
lightly trimmed of fat
(4 pieces)

Special equipment
Fine strainer (chinois)

Preparation time
10 minutes

Cooking time
20 minutes

Peel and slice the shallots. Melt the butter in a small saucepan over medium–high heat. Add the shallots and cook for 1–2 minutes. Pour in the wine and boil, stirring, for 30 seconds to deglaze the pan. Cook until the liquid is reduced by a quarter, then add the cream and strong and wholegrain mustards. Reduce the heat to low, season with salt and pepper and gently simmer until the sauce is smooth and has thickened slightly. Strain the mustard cream into another saucepan or bowl and keep warm in a bain-marie (water bath).

Heat the oil in a large frying pan over high heat. Season the steak with salt and pepper, add to the pan and cook until rare, medium or well-done, according to your taste.

Serve the steaks with the mustard cream on the side.

Suggestion
Serve with crispy potato chips (p. 238).

PASTRAMI SANDWICHES

Makes 4 sandwiches

4 tablespoons mayonnaise

4 tablespoons dijon mustard

8 thick slices country-style bread

350 g (12 oz) thinly sliced pastrami

250 g (9 oz) sauerkraut, warmed (optional)

4 gherkins (pickles)

Preparation time
10 minutes

Cooking time
5 minutes

Preheat the oven to 180°C (350°F).

Combine the mayonnaise with the mustard and spread this mixture generously onto 4 slices of the bread. Top with sauerkraut (if using) and/or pastrami. Brush the remaining 4 slices of bread with the mayonnaise and mustard mixture and place on top of the pastrami. Press down gently on the sandwiches, cut them in half and arrange on a baking tray. Put them in the oven for 5 minutes to warm through, without browning.

Serve warm with salad, crispy potato chips (p. 238) and gherkins.

Variations
You can replace the pastrami with very thin slices of roast beef or dried beef (such as bresaola).

SHREDDED BEEF SALAD

Serves 4–6

1 handful dill

1 handful
coriander (cilantro)

150 g (5½ oz) cherry
tomatoes

1 small Lebanese (short)
cucumber (about
150 g/5½ oz)

1 onion

700 g (1 lb 9 oz) cooked
beef, such as leftover
pot-au-feu

120 ml (3¾ oz)
sunflower oil

4 tablespoons white
wine vinegar

Special equipment
Toaster

Preparation time
25 minutes

Wash and chop the dill and coriander leaves. Halve the cherry tomatoes and cut the cucumber into small chunks. Peel and finely chop the onion. Shred the meat and place on a platter with the herbs, tomatoes and cucumber.

Make a vinaigrette by whisking together the oil, vinegar and some salt and pepper in a small bowl or cup. Drizzle over the beef salad and gently combine.

Suggestion
Serve with toasted country-style bread.

KOFTAS WITH SPICES, CORIANDER AND ROCKET

Serves 6–8

2 handfuls coriander (cilantro)

600 g (1 lb 5 oz) minced (ground) beef

1 tablespoon ground cumin

1 tablespoon curry powder

2 baguettes, to serve

100 g (3½ oz) rocket (arugula), to serve

2 tablespoons olive oil

Special equipment
Skewers

Preparation time
30 minutes

Resting time
30 minutes

Cooking time
10 minutes

If using wooden skewers, soak them in water until ready to use.

Wash the coriander and chop the leaves coarsely.

Put the minced meat in a large bowl. Season with salt and pepper and add the chopped coriander, cumin and curry powder. Add a little water and knead with your hands to mix well.

Divide the meat between the skewers, lightly pressing it onto the skewer so it remains in place. Put on a plate and cover with plastic wrap. Rest the koftas for 30 minutes in the refrigerator.

Preheat the barbecue or grill (broiler) to high. Cook the koftas for 6–8 minutes, until cooked through.

To serve, cut the baguettes lengthways and then into pieces. Dress the rocket with the olive oil. Pull the skewers out of the koftas and fill the bread with the meat and rocket.

Suggestion
Serve with crispy potato chips (p. 238).

SHABU-SHABU (JAPANESE FONDUE)

Serves 4

200 g (7 oz) firm tofu

20 baby spinach leaves

2 shiitake mushrooms

¼ Chinese cabbage (wong bok)

1 litre (35 fl oz/4 cups) dashi (made with dashi powder, available from Asian food stores)

500 g (1 lb 2 oz) wagyu beef, thinly sliced as for a carpaccio

Special equipment
Table stove

Small earthenware pot

Preparation time
20 minutes

Cooking time
20 minutes

Cut the tofu into small pieces. Wash and dry the baby spinach and mushrooms. Finely slice the Chinese cabbage.

Lay out all the ingredients on the table.

Light the table stove and place the earthenware pot over the flame. Pour in the dashi and bring to the boil. Add the cabbage, mushrooms and tofu and let them cook for 8 minutes.

Each person is given their own small bowl and chopsticks. To eat, dip slices of meat into the broth for a few seconds using the chopsticks and transfer to your own bowl with some tofu, cabbage and baby spinach leaves.

FLANK STEAK WITH CRISPY SHALLOTS

Serves 4

1 handful flat-leaf parsley

5 French shallots

Oil for deep-frying

3 tablespoons
sunflower oil

50 g (1¾ oz) butter

500 g (1 lb 2oz) flank
(bavette) steak in
1 whole piece

Special equipment
Deep-fryer
or large saucepan

Preparation time
15 minutes

Cooking time
20 minutes

Meat resting time
5 minutes

Pick the parsley leaves and wash, dry and chop them. Set aside.

Peel and thinly slice the shallots. Heat the oil for deep-frying to 160°C (315°F) (when a cube of bread tiurns golden-brown in 30–35 seconds). Deep-fry the shallot slices for 1–2 minutes, or until golden and crispy. Drain them on paper towel and keep warm.

Heat the sunflower oil and butter in a large frying pan over medium–high heat. Season the steak with salt and pepper and cook for 3 minutes on one side. Turn the steak, reduce the heat to medium–low and cook for a further 5 minutes. Remove the pan from the heat and drain the meat on a board. Cover the steak with foil and let it rest for 5 minutes, turning once.

To serve, cut the steak into 4 slices and put on individual plates. Reheat the cooking juices in the pan, add the chopped parsley and stir through. Pour the juices and parsley over the meat and scatter over the crispy shallots.

Suggestion
Serve with crispy potato chips (p. 238) or a potato purée (p. 254).

BRAISED BEEF AND CARROTS

Serves 4–6

2 rashers bacon
or 2 slices speck

2 large onions

10 large carrots

4 garlic cloves

4 tablespoons olive oil

3 beef cheeks or
1.2 kg/2 lb 11 oz stewing
beef (such as blade,
chuck or shin)

2 sprigs thyme

2 bay leaves

1 teaspoon sel gris (coarse
grey sea salt) or other
coarse sea salt

Special equipment
Cast-iron casserole dish
with lid

Preparation time
30 minutes

Cooking time
2 hours 10 minutes

Cut the bacon or speck into large dice. Peel and chop the onions. Peel the carrots and slice into fairly thick rounds. Bruise the garlic cloves in their skin.

Heat the oil in a large cast-iron casserole dish over high heat. Season the beef with salt and pepper. Cook the beef, bacon and onions for 2–3 minutes. Add the carrots, garlic, thyme and bay leaves and stir through. Add enough water to just cover the meat and vegetables. Cover, reduce the heat to low and simmer for 2 hours.

Once the meat is cooked and tender, bring the casserole dish straight to the table and serve hot.

Suggestion
You can prepare this dish the day before.

STEAMED MEATBALLS WITH CORIANDER AND CUMIN

Serves 4

2 handfuls
coriander (cilantro)

700 g (1 lb 9 oz) minced
(ground) beef

2 tablespoons
cumin seeds

1 teaspoon curry powder

1 tablespoon fish sauce

1 teaspoon sesame oil

1 teaspoon rice vinegar

Special equipment

Large double saucepan
or bamboo steamer

Preparation time

20 minutes

Resting time

1 hour

Cooking time

5 minutes

Wash and dry the coriander. Pick and coarsely chop the leaves.

Put the beef, coriander, cumin seeds, curry powder, fish sauce, sesame oil and rice vinegar in a large bowl. Add 2 tablespoons cold water, season with salt and pepper and knead together with your fingers to combine all the ingredients well. Shape the mixture into large meatballs. Put them on a large plate, cover with plastic wrap and refrigerate for 1 hour.

Bring a saucepan of water to the boil and place the meatballs in the top of a double saucepan or a bamboo steamer. Steam the meatballs for 2–3 minutes (the middle should stay raw), then arrange them on individual plates.

Suggestion

Serve hot or cold with crispy potato chips (p. 238).

BEEF CARPACCIO WITH SHAVED TOMME CHEESE

Serves 4

8 basil leaves

4 portions of beef carpaccio (prepared by the butcher)

200 g (7 oz) tomme de Savoie cheese, or use cantal, comte or gruyère

4 tablespoons olive or walnut oil

Special equipment
A good paring knife

Preparation time
10 minutes

Wash, dry and finely chop the basil. Divide the beef between 4 plates.

Use a sharp knife to make thin, even shavings of cheese, and divide them between the plates of carpaccio. Season with salt and pepper, drizzle with a little olive or walnut oil and scatter over the basil.

Suggestion
Serve with toasted slices of country-style bread.

BEEF AND GRAVY PIES

Serves 4

600 g (1 lb 5 oz) stewing beef, such as gravy beef

2 carrots

2 onions

2 garlic cloves

25 g (1 oz) butter

400 ml (14 fl oz) brown veal stock

2 pinches of thyme leaves

For the pastry

250 g (9 oz) plain (all-purpose) flour

110 g (3¾ oz) butter

2–3 tablespoons water

1 pinch salt

Special equipment

Rolling pin

4 small pie tins or ramekins, 7 cm (2¾ in) in diameter

Preparation time

45 minutes

Resting time

1 hour

Cooking time

1 hour

To make the pastry, combine all the ingredients and bring together into a ball. Wrap in plastic wrap and put in the refrigerator for 1 hour.

Meanwhile, cut the beef into small cubes. Peel and chop the carrots and onions into a fine dice. Peel and crush the garlic.

Heat the butter in a large saucepan with a heavy base. Cook the beef, carrot and onion for 5 minutes. Add the stock, crushed garlic and thyme. Season with salt and pepper. Reduce the heat to low and cook for 25 minutes. Set aside to cool completely.

Preheat the oven to 140°C (275°F).

Roll out the pastry and cut out 4 circles, 10 cm (4 in) in diameter. Place in the base of the pie tins. Gather together the leftover pastry and roll it out again. Fill the tins with the meat mixture and top the pies with the remaining pastry, pinching the edges together to seal the pastry well.

Cook in the preheated oven for 15 minutes, then increase the temperature to 180°C (350°F) and cook for a further 10 minutes, or until the pies are cooked through and golden brown on top. Serve immediately.

Suggestion

Serve with potato purée (p. 254).

BEEF TENDERLOIN WITH BLUE CHEESE AND BACON

Serves 4

200 g (7 oz) blue cheese

2 thick rashers bacon or
2 thick slices speck

2 tablespoons
sunflower oil

50 g (1¾ oz) butter

4 tenderloin beef steaks,
about 200 g (7 oz) each

Preparation time
5 minutes

Cooking time
6–8 minutes

Cut the blue cheese into small pieces and set them aside on a plate in the refrigerator. Trim the bacon of rind, excess fat and any hard cartilage, then cut into thin strips. Blanch the bacon for 10 minutes in a saucepan of boiling water, then drain and let it dry.

Heat the oil and butter in a large frying pan over medium–high heat. Season the steaks with salt and pepper and cook for 3–4 minutes on each side.

Transfer the steaks to individual plates and add the bacon to the pan. Cook until browned and divide the hot bacon pieces and pieces of blue cheese between the steaks.

Suggestion
Serve immediately with a green salad and oven-baked skin-on chips (p. 298).

ARMENIAN BEEF PIZZA

Serves 6

For the dough

21 g (¾ oz) fresh yeast

500 g (1 lb 2 oz) plain (all-purpose) flour

4 tablespoons olive oil

2 pinches salt

For the topping

4 sprigs flat-leaf parsley

3 garlic cloves

1 capsicum (pepper)

2 tomatoes

1 onion

2 tablespoons olive oil

1 teaspoon tomato paste (concentrated purée)

1 teaspoon chilli powder

600 g (1 lb 5 oz) minced (ground) beef

Lemon wedges, to serve

Chopped mint, to garnish

Preparation time
45 minutes

Resting time
1 hour 40 minutes

Cooking time
15 minutes

To make the pizza dough, blend the yeast with a little lukewarm water and combine with the flour in a large mixing bowl. Knead the dough with your fingertips, adding a little water until the dough is smooth and firm. Place a damp cloth over the bowl, then let it rest for 1 hour 40 minutes in a warm place (the dough should double in volume).

Meanwhile, to make the pizza sauce, wash the parsley and pick off the leaves. Peel the garlic cloves, de-stem and seed the capsicum, seed the tomatoes and peel the onion. Chop all of these ingredients into small pieces in a food processor, then blend them with the olive oil, tomato paste and chilli powder.

Dust a work surface with a little flour. Divide the dough into 6 equal pieces. Roll out the pieces of dough with a rolling pin into 6 pizzas, each about 25 cm across.

Preheat the oven to 250°C (500°F). Line pizza trays or baking trays with baking paper.

Transfer the pizza bases to the pizza trays or baking trays. Spread the pizza sauce over the base of the pizzas, leaving 2 cm (¾ inch) around the edge. Spread the minced meat over the whole surface of the pizzas, packing it down well with your hand.

Drizzle with the olive oil and sprinkle with the salt. Bake the pizzas, 3 at a time, for about 15 minutes, or until cooked and golden. Serve hot or warm with a squeeze of lemon. Scatter over the mint to garnish.

BEEF AND FOIE GRAS PIES

Serves 4

1 handful chives

4 prunes

500 g (1 lb 2 oz) leftover cooked beef from a pot-au-feu or bourguignon

200 g (7 oz) foie gras (or chicken liver pâté)

4 tablespoons armagnac (or use cognac or brandy)

1 egg

2 sheets (25 x 50 cm/ 10 x 20 inches) frozen puff pastry, thawed

2 egg yolks

Preparation time
30 minutes

Cooking time
35 minutes

Wash and chop the chives. Soak the prunes in a bowl of lukewarm water. Shred the meat, cut the foie gras into small cubes and the prunes into small pieces.

Combine the pieces of prune with the meat, the foie gras, armagnac, whole egg and chives in a mixing bowl. Season with salt and pepper and set aside in the refrigerator.

Preheat the oven to 180°C (350°F). Line a baking tray with a sheet of baking paper.

Make 8 circles of puff pastry, about 15 cm (6 inches) in diameter. Whisk the egg yolks with a little water in a bowl. Lay 4 circles of dough on a work surface and divide the filling between them, placing it in the centre. Brush the edges with a little water, place the other circles of dough on top, then press the two edges together to seal the pastry and form small pies. Place them on the prepared baking tray. Whisk the egg yolks lightly and brush over the pies. Bake the pies for 35 minutes, or until browned on top and cooked through.

Suggestion
Enjoy the pies hot with a green salad.

BEEF RIBS IN APPLE BARBECUE SAUCE

Serves 4

4 French shallots

2 tablespoons apple sauce

3 tablespoons tomato sauce (ketchup)

100 ml (3½ fl oz) soy sauce

A few drops Tabasco sauce

1 teaspoon ground cinnamon

1 teaspoon ground paprika

100 ml (3½ fl oz) apple juice

3 tablespoons cider vinegar

1 teaspoon raw (demerara) sugar

16 beef short ribs or rib ends

4 tablespoons peanut oil

Preparation time
30 minutes

Resting time
Overnight

Cooking time
3 hours

The day before, peel and chop the shallots. In a large baking dish, combine the shallots, apple sauce, tomato sauce, soy sauce, Tabasco, cinnamon, paprika, apple juice, vinegar and sugar. Season with salt and pepper. Add the beef ribs and stir to coat well. Cover and marinate overnight in the refrigerator.

On the day, preheat the oven to 170°C (325°F).

Heat the oil in a large frying pan over medium–high heat. Remove the ribs from the marinade and brown them on all sides in the pan. Return the ribs to the baking dish with the marinade and cook in the oven for 3 hours. Add a little water from time to time when the marinade reduces.

Once the ribs are cooked and meltingly tender, remove from the oven and set aside to cool a little. Serve.

Suggestion
Enjoy the beef ribs coated in sauce with potato crisps (p. 242).

JUMBO RAVIOLI WITH SHREDDED BEEF AND FOIE GRAS

Serves 4

700 g (1 lb 9 oz) leftover beef from pot-au-feu or another braised dish

300 g (10½ oz) foie gras (or chicken liver pâté)

3 egg yolks

2 tablespoons port

300 ml (10½ fl oz) pot-au-feu broth

100 ml (3½ fl oz) thin (pouring) cream

24 ready-made pasta wrappers or wonton wrappers (sold in Asian food stores)

Special equipment
Pastry brush

Stick (hand) blender

Preparation time
45 minutes

Resting time
20 minutes

Cooking time
20 minutes

Shred the meat and set it aside. Dice the foie gras. Whisk the egg yolks with a little water. Lay out 12 ravioli wrappers on your work surface and brush with the egg yolk mixture. Divide the meat and foie gras between them, placing on the centre of the wrappers. Cover with the 12 remaining wrappers, then press around the edges with your fingertips to seal them well. Refrigerate for 20 minutes.

Meanwhile, combine the port with the broth in a medium saucepan and reduce by a quarter over high heat. Add the cream and cook, whisking, until the sauce thickens. Remove from the heat, season with salt and pepper and blend with a stick blender. Set aside and keep warm.

Bring a large saucepan of salted water to the boil over high heat. Cook the ravioli, several at a time, for 5 minutes. Drain and divide them between deep plates. Pour on some of the reserved sauce and serve immediately.

ASIAN-STYLE STEAK TARTARE

Serves 4

10 Thai basil leaves

10 mint leaves

½ handful coriander
(cilantro)

4 lemongrass stems,
pale part only

700 g (1 lb 9 oz) minced
(ground) beef

2 tablespoons
Japanese-style soy sauce

2 tablespoons toasted
sesame seeds

100 ml (3½ fl oz)
olive oil

2 tablespoons sesame oil

1 teaspoon Asian chilli
sauce or 3 drops
Tabasco sauce

Preparation time
25 minutes

Wash, dry and roughly chop the Thai basil, mint and coriander. Finely chop the lemongrass stems.

In a large bowl, combine the meat with the soy sauce, sesame seeds, olive oil, sesame oil and chilli sauce. Season with salt and pepper, mix together vigorously, then add the chopped herbs and lemongrass.

Suggestion
Serve with crispy potato chips (p. 238).

PEPPER STEAK

Serves 4

4 thick tenderloin steaks (chateaubriand), about 200 g (7 oz) each

2 tablespoons cracked black pepper

80 g (2¾ oz) butter

1 tablespoon sunflower oil

30 ml (1 fl oz) whiskey

100 ml (3½ fl oz) crème fraîche

5 peppercorn mix, cracked, to serve

Preparation time
15 minutes

Cooking time
25 minutes

Season the steaks normally with salt. Scatter over the cracked black pepper and press onto the meat. Melt the butter and oil in a large frying pan over medium–high heat. Cook the steaks for 2 minutes on each side then transfer to a large plate.

Add the whiskey to the frying pan and light with a flame (flambé). Cook for 20 seconds to reduce the sauce then add the crème fraîche. Cook for 3 minutes, stirring with a wooden spatula, until the sauce thickens slightly. Reduce the heat to medium, return the steaks to the sauce and reheat in the sauce for 30 seconds. Adjust the seasoning and sprinkle with cracked 5 peppercorn mix.

Suggestion

Serve hot with potato crisps (p. 242) or sautéed potatoes with basil and olives (p. 282).

RUMP STEAK WITH FRESH GRAPE AND SPINACH SALAD

Serves 4–6

200 g (7 oz) red grapes, not too large

200 g (7 oz) baby spinach leaves

4 tablespoons olive oil

2 tablespoons balsamic vinegar

1 thick slice rump steak, about 900 g (2 lb)

Preparation time
10 minutes

Cooking time
6 minutes

Meat resting time
4 minutes

Separate the grapes from the bunch and wash them. Wash and dry the baby spinach leaves.

Whisk the oil and balsamic together in a medium bowl. Set aside.

Season the meat with salt and pepper. Heat a large non-stick frying pan over high heat. Sear the meat for 3 minutes on each side in the dry pan. Transfer to a plate, cover with foil and let it rest for 4 minutes. Cut the steak into slices.

Add the cooking juices to the oil and balsamic mixture. Combine the grapes with the spinach, dress with the vinaigrette and place on serving plates. Top with the steak and serve immediately.

BEEF AND WILD MUSHROOM PIE

Serves 4

1 handful chives

200 g (7 oz) cep
(porcini) mushrooms

150 g (5½ oz) chanterelle
mushrooms

150 g (5½ oz) black
trumpet mushrooms

2 tablespoons pistachio
nut kernels

10 walnuts

50 g (1¾ oz) butter

1 tablespoon walnut oil

1 tablespoon sunflower oil

600 g (1 lb 5 oz) minced
(ground) beef

4 tablespoons port

2 eggs

2 sheets (25 x 50 cm/
10 x 20 inches) frozen
puff pastry, thawed

2 egg yolks

Preparation time
45 minutes

Cooking time
35 minutes

Wash and chop the chives. Wash and dry the ceps, then cut them into pieces. Clean the chanterelles and black trumpets. Roughly chop the pistachios and walnuts.

Heat the butter and oils in a medium frying pan over medium–high heat unti foaming. Add the ceps and cook for 10 minutes, stirring. Add the chanterelles and black trumpets and cook for 5 minutes, stirring. Drain the mushrooms.

In a large bowl, combine the minced beef, port, whole eggs, cooked mushrooms, chives, pistachios, walnuts and port. Season with salt and pepper and mix well.

Preheat the oven to 180°C (350°F). Line a baking tray with a sheet of baking paper.

Cut each pastry sheet into a large circle. Lay the first circle of pastry on a work surface and place the filling in the centre. Brush the edge with a little water, place the other circle of pastry on top and press down the edge to seal the two pieces together.

Transfer the pie to the baking tray. Whisk the egg yolks and brush over the top of the pie. Bake for 35 minutes, or until golden and cooked through.

Suggestion

When in season, fresh wild European cep (porcini), chanterelle and black trumpet mushrooms may be available at gourmet food shops. Otherwise, use fresh locally cultivated mushrooms of choice, such as shiitake, oyster and wood ear, or wild pine mushrooms.

WARM BEEF RICE PAPER ROLLS

Serves 4

400 g (14 oz) beef for pan-frying (inside round, rump, tenderloin or striploin)

2 tablespoons olive oil

1 large handful mint

1 large handful coriander (cilantro)

a selection of vegetables, including lettuce, carrot, capsicum (pepper), diakon and spring onion (scallion)

8 small rice paper wrappers

For the sauce

30 g (1 oz) peanuts

1 handful coriander (cilantro)

5 mint leaves

30 g (1 oz) ginger

3 tablespoons olive oil

2 tablespoons soy sauce

Preparation time
35 minutes

Cooking time
10 minutes

To make the sauce, toast the peanuts in a dry frying pan and set them aside. Wash and dry the mint and coriander and peel the ginger. Blend all of the sauce ingredients in a food processor and set aside.

Cut the meat into small slices. Heat 1 tablespoon of the olive oil in a large frying pan over medium–high heat. Cook the meat, tossing frequently, for 2–3 minutes. Set aside and keep warm.

Wash, dry and shred the mint, coriander leaves and vegetables.

Dip the rice paper wrappers in lukewarm water, drain and lay out on a work surface. Divide the meat, mint, coriander and vegetables between the wrappers, season with salt and pepper and roll up tightly. Serve with the sauce.

BRAISED OXTAIL WITH RED WINE

Serves 6

4 French shallots

2 garlic cloves

50 g (1¾ oz) butter

2 tablespoons
sunflower oil

500 g (1 lb 2 oz) oxtail

600 g (1 lb 5 oz) carrots,
peeled and sliced
into rounds

1 large sprig thyme

1 bay leaf

1 tablespoon plain
(all-purpose) flour

750 ml (26 fl oz/3 cups)
red wine

500 ml (17 fl oz/2 cups)
beef broth or brown
veal stock

Preparation time
35 minutes

Cooking time
2 hours 15 minutes

Peel and chop the shallots and garlic. Heat the butter and oil in a casserole dish over medium–high heat. Season the pieces of oxtail with salt and pepper. Cook the meat and carrots until well browned.

Add the chopped shallots and garlic, thyme and bay leaf to the dish and cook for a 2–3 minutes. Add the flour and red wine and stir to blend. Reduce the heat to medium–low and cook until the liquid is reduced by half.

Add the broth or stock and 400 ml (14 fl oz) water, reduce the heat to low and simmer for 2 hours, stirring occasionally.

Once the meat is cooked and meltingly tender, remove from the heat and adjust the seasoning.

Suggestion
Serve with potato purée (p. 254).

BEEF CARPACCIO WITH BASIL AND PARMESAN

Serves 4

1 large handful basil

100 g (3½ oz) good
parmesan cheese

500 g (1 lb 2 oz)
beef tenderloin

4 tablespoons olive oil

Special equipment
Large knife

Preparation time
25 minutes

Wash and dry the basil leaves. Cut them into small pieces with a pair of scissors. Cut the parmesan into slivers.

Slice the meat thinly, but not too thinly, with a large well-sharpened knife, then arrange the slices on 4 plates.

Sprinkle with the chopped basil and parmesan slivers, season with salt and pepper and drizzle over the olive oil.

Suggestion
Serve with slices of toasted bread.

HANGER STEAK WITH CARAMELISED BABY ONIONS

Serves 4

250 g (9 oz) baby onions

130 g (4½ oz) butter

2 teaspoons caster (superfine) sugar

2 tablespoons sunflower oil

4 hanger (thick skirt) steaks, about 200 g (7 oz) each

50 ml (1½ fl oz) port

Preparation time
25 minutes

Cooking time
25 minutes

Peel the baby onions. Melt 80 g (2¾ oz) of the butter in a large frying pan over medium–high heat. Add the onions and cook for 1–2 minutes. Add the sugar and add water to reach halfway up the onions. Cook until the liquid has evaporated, then caramelise the onions, stirring, so they brown all over.

Heat the oil and the remaining 50 g (1¾ oz) of butter in a large frying pan. Season the steaks with salt and pepper, add to the pan and cook for 1–2 minutes each side, or until done to your liking. Pour in the port and boil, stirring, for 30 seconds to deglaze the pan. Allow to boil and to reduce the liquid by a quarter, then add the caramelised onions and mix together.

Suggestion
Serve hot with potato purée (p. 254).

SUMMERTIME BEEF SALAD

Serves 4–6

1 small handful dill

1 handful basil

5 fairly firm tomatoes

4 small organic cucumbers

700 g (1 lb 9 oz) beef for pan-frying (inside round, rump, tenderloin or striploin)

160 ml (5¼ fl oz) olive oil

2 tablespoons red or white wine vinegar

2 pinches ground cumin

Preparation time
25 minutes

Cooking time
10 minutes

Wash and chop the dill and basil leaves. Wash and de-stem the tomatoes, then cut them in half. Remove the seeds with a spoon, then chop the flesh into small dice. Cut the cucumbers lengthways, remove the seeds and cut the flesh into matchsticks.

Ten minutes before serving time, season the steaks with salt and pepper. Heat 2 tablespoons of the olive oil in a large frying pan over medium–high heat. Cook the steaks for 2–3 minutes on each side, according to the doneness you like, then drain them on a wooden board. Pour the cooking juices into a large bowl.

Finely dice the meat and add to the bowl with the remaining olive oil, the vinegar, cumin, tomatoes and cucumber sticks. Toss to combine. Add the dill and basil and toss through. Adjust the seasoning and serve immediately.

INDIAN-STYLE BEEF CURRY

Serves 4

2 lemongrass stems,
white part only

4 garlic cloves

2 onions

1 large handful
coriander (cilantro)

4 tablespoons
sunflower oil

1.5 kg (3 lb 5 oz) stewing
beef (blade, chuck or
shin), cut into large cubes

2 tablespoons
curry powder

1 teaspoon ground cumin

2 cloves

1 cinnamon stick

500 ml (17 fl oz/2 cups)
coconut milk

100 ml (3½ fl oz) beef
broth or brown veal stock

50 g (1¾ oz) large raisins

Special equipment
Large cast-iron casserole
dish (with lid)

Preparation time
10 minutes

Cooking time
2 hours

Trim, peel and slice the lemongrass, using the white part only. Peel and chop the garlic. Peel and slice the onions. Wash the coriander, keeping the stems, and set aside.

Heat the oil in a large cast-iron casserole dish over high heat. Cook the beef on all sides until browned. Add the lemongrass, garlic, onion, curry powder, cumin, cloves and cinnamon and cook, stirring, for 5 minutes. Add the coconut milk and stock, stir through and reduce the heat to low. Gently simmer for 2 hours, or until the meat is tender and cooked through.

Add the coriander and raisins, and serve immediately.

BEEF AND CARROTS WITH CUMIN AND BASIL

Serves 4

8 large carrots

2 large onions

4 garlic cloves

1 large handful basil

4 tablespoons olive oil

1.3 kg (3 lb) stewing beef, (blade, chuck or shin), in large pieces

2 bay leaves

2 tablespoons cumin seeds

2 teaspoons coarse sea salt

Special equipment

Large cast-iron casserole dish (with lid)

Preparation time

30 minutes

Cooking time

2 hours

Peel the carrots and slice into fairly thick rounds. Peel and chop the onions. Bruise the garlic cloves in their skin. Wash the basil leaves and set aside.

Heat the oil in a casserole dish over high heat. Season the meat with salt and pepper then add to the pan. Add the onions and cook, stirring, for 2–3 minutes, or until starting to brown. Add the bruised garlic cloves, bay leaves, cumin seeds and carrots.

Add water just to the top of the meat and vegetables. Add the coarse sea salt, stir through and cover the dish. Reduce the heat to low and simmer for 2 hours.

Once the meat is cooked and tender, add the basil leaves, then serve hot, directly from the casserole dish.

RUMP STEAK WITH BLUE CHEESE SAUCE

Serves 4

200 g (7 oz) blue cheese

250 ml (9 fl oz/1 cup) thin (pouring) cream

1 thick piece (about 1 kg/2 lb 4 oz) good-quality rump steak, cut along the whole length of the rump

3 tablespoons olive oil

4 small butter or romaine lettuces

3 sprigs thyme

Special equipment
1 good paring knife

Preparation time
25 minutes

Cooking time
10 minutes

Meat resting time
4 minutes

Cut the blue cheese into cubes. Pour the cream into a small saucepan over medium heat and bring to the boil. Add the pieces of blue cheese and season with salt and pepper. Remove the saucepan from the heat and stir to melt the cheese. Set aside the pan, keeping the sauce warm.

Fifteen minutes before serving time, heat a large dry frying pan over high heat. Season the meat with salt and pepper and cook for 3 minutes on both sides. Drain the meat on a board, cover it with foil and let it rest for 2 minutes on each side.

Meanwhile, heat the olive oil in the same frying pan over high heat. Cut each of the lettuces into quarters, season with salt and pepper and cook for 4 minutes, turning often. Add the thyme and remove from the heat.

Arrange the lettuce and thyme on a large serving plate. Cut the meat into thin slices and serve with the blue cheese sauce and crispy potato chips (p. 238).

PULLED-BEEF BUNS

Makes 4

2 carrots

700 g (1 lb 9 oz) leftover braised beef (such as provençal, bourguignon or beef cheek)

4 gherkins (pickles)

1 small handful chives

4 hamburger buns

2 tablespoons strong mustard

4 slices pancetta

200 ml (7 fl oz) cooking juices from the braised beef

Preparation time
25 minutes

Cooking time
15 minutes

Grate the carrots. Shred the beef and set aside. Slice the gherkins. Wash and chop the chives.

Fifteen minutes before serving time, cut the buns in half and toast them lightly in the oven. Brush the cut sides with the mustard.

Cut the slices of pancetta in half and brown them in a dry frying pan over medium–high heat. Transfer to a plate. Heat the shredded beef in the same frying pan.

Fill the buns with the pancetta, gherkins, carrot and shredded beef.

Arrange the sandwiches on individual plates. Bring the cooking juices to the boil in a small saucepan over high heat. Pour over the buns, sprinkle with chives and serve immediately.

Suggestion
Serve very hot with crispy potato chips (p. 238).

BEEF STEW WITH OLIVES AND ORANGE

Serves 4–6

1 orange

1 large onion

5 garlic cloves

2 tablespoons
sunflower oil

1.2 kg (2 lb 11 oz)
stewing beef (blade,
chuck or shin),
cut into large cubes

150 g (5½ oz) green olives

2 sprigs thyme

750 ml (26 fl oz/3 cups)
white wine

500 ml (17 fl oz/2 cups)
beef broth or brown
veal stock

Special equipment
Zester

Citrus juicer

Preparation time
30 minutes

Cooking time
3 hours 15 minutes

Zest and juice the orange. Peel and slice the onion. Bruise the garlic in its skin. Heat the oil in a large casserole dish over medium–high heat. Cook the beef until browned on all sides.

Drain off the fat, then add the orange zest, onion, garlic, olives and thyme. Cook for 15 minutes, stirring, or until browned. Add the wine, orange juice and stock. Bring to the boil, skim any fat from the surface and season with salt and pepper. Cover, reduce the heat to low and simmer for 3 hours, or until the meat is meltingly tender.

Adjust the seasoning to taste and serve hot, directly from the casserole dish.

STEAK TARTARE WITH PARMESAN, TRUFFLES AND OLIVE OIL

Serves 4

80 g (2¾ oz) shaved parmesan cheese

25 g (1 oz) truffle slices

700 g (1 lb 9 oz) minced (ground) beef

3 tablespoons truffle oil

3 tablespoon good-quality olive oil

Special equipment
1 good paring knife

Preparation time
15 minutes

Set aside some shaved parmesan for garnishing, and roughly chop the remainder. Drain the truffle slices. Combine the minced meat with the truffle oil and olive oil in a large bowl. Season with salt and pepper, add the chopped parmesan and mix again vigorously.

Divide the tartare between 4 serving plates. Top with truffle slices and a little parmesan. Serve with hot toast.

Serves 4–6

5 garlic cloves

100 ml (3½ fl oz) olive oil

1.2 kg (2 lb 11 oz) stewing beef (blade, chuck or shin), cut into large cubes

1 large sprig thyme

1 bay leaf

100 ml (3½ fl oz) white wine

1 tablespoon plain (all-purpose) flour

70 g (2½ oz) tomato paste (concentrated purée)

100 g (3½ oz) baby spinach leaves

1 small handful tarragon

1 handful basil

100 g (3½ oz) green beans

200 g (7 oz) shelled peas

12 small spring carrots

10 small spring turnips

100 g (3½ oz) snow peas (mangetout)

12 asparagus spears

200 g (7 oz) podded broad beans

Preparation time
35 minutes

Cooking time
1 hour 30 minutes

BEEF STEW WITH SPRING VEGETABLES

Bruise the garlic cloves in their skin.

Heat 4 tablespoons of the olive oil in a large cast-iron casserole dish over high heat. Add the beef and cook for 2–3 minutes, or until browned. Season with salt and pepper. Add the garlic, thyme and bay leaf and cook for 1–2 minutes. Pour in the wine and boil, stirring, for 30 seconds to deglaze the dish. Let the liquid reduce then add the flour and tomato paste. Stir through and add 250 ml (9 fl oz/1 cup) hot water. Reduce the heat to low and simmer for 1 hour 15 minutes.

Meanwhile, wash the baby spinach, tarragon and basil leaves. Trim the green beans and snow peas. Peel the carrots and turnips.

Bring a large saucepan with salted water to the boil over high heat. Add the baby spinach, tarragon, basil, green beans and snow peas, reduce the heat to medium–low and cook until tender. Trim the lower part of the asparagus spears. Add the asparagus to the saucepan and simmer for 2 minutes.

Once the meat is well cooked and tender, add all of the vegetables and aromatics to the casserole dish, plus the remaining spoon of olive oil. Adjust the seasoning, gently stir and serve directly from the casserole dish.

CHILLI CON CARNE

Serves 4–6

4 garlic cloves

2 large onions

4 tablespoons sunflower oil

1.5 kg (3 lb 5 oz) stewing beef (blade, chuck or shin), cut into large cubes

2 mild chillies

1 tablespoon tomato paste (concentrated purée)

200 ml (7 fl oz) beef broth or brown veal stock

1 teaspoon chilli powder

800 g (1 lb 12 oz) tinned red kidney beans, drained

Preparation time
25 minutes

Cooking time
2 hours 30 minutes

Peel and chop the garlic cloves and onions.

Heat the oil in a large casserole dish over medium–high. Add the beef and cook or 2–3 minutes, or until browned on all sides. Add the garlic, onion and whole chillies and cook, stirring, for 2–3 minutes. Add the tomato paste and beef broth and bring to the boil. Season with salt and pepper and add the chilli powder. Reduce the heat to low, cover and simmer for 2 hours 30 minutes. Add the kidney beans halfway through the cooking time.

Once the meat is meltingly tender, adjust the seasoning and serve hot with steamed potatoes.

Suggestion
For a quicker dish, you can replace the stewing beef with the same quantity of minced beef.

CLASSIC STEAK TARTARE

Serves 4

1 garlic clove

2 large French shallots

10 sprigs flat-leaf parsley

10 g (¼ oz) capers, chopped

7 cornichons (small gherkins/pickles)

1 small handful chives

600 g (1 lb 5 oz) minced (ground) beef

1 tablespoon dijon mustard

4 egg yolks

3 tablespoons tomato sauce (ketchup)

5 drops Tabasco sauce

1 tablespoon mayonnaise (optional)

Preparation time
25 minutes

Peel and chop the garlic and shallots. Wash and chop the parsley leaves. Chop the capers and cornichons. Wash and chop the chives.

Combine all of the ingredients. Season with salt and pepper to taste.

Suggestion
Serve this tartare chilled with crispy potato chips (p. 238) or chilli potatoes (p. 310).

STEAK TARTARE SALAD

Serves 4

2 onions

10 sprigs flat-leaf parsley

200 g (7 oz) rocket (arugula)

700 g (1 lb 9 oz) minced (ground) beef

100 g (3½ oz) tomato sauce (ketchup)

4 tablespoons olive oil, plus 1 tablespoon extra to dress the salad

2 tablespoons Japanese-style soy sauce

2 drops Tabasco sauce

Preparation time

15 minutes

Peel and chop the onions. Wash and chop the parsley leaves. Wash and dry the rocket.

Combine the minced meat with the tomato sauce, the 4 tablespoons olive oil and the soy sauce in a large bowl. Add the onion, parsley and Tabasco and mix well. Season with salt and pepper.

Divide the rocket between 4 plates and drizzle over the extra olive oil. Top with the tartare and serve chilled.

Suggestion

Serve this tartare with soufflé potatoes (p. 250) or potato crisps (p. 242).

TOMATOES STUFFED WITH BEEF AND SPICY SAUSAGES

Serves 4

4 merguez (spicy lamb) sausages

1 teaspoon dried thyme

1 egg

500 g (1 lb 2 oz) minced (ground) beef

8 small tomatoes

4 tablespoons olive oil

Preparation time
25 minutes

Cooking time
20 minutes

Preheat the oven to 180°C (350°F).

Skin the merguez and combine the sausage meat in a large bowl with the dried thyme, egg and minced beef. Season with salt and pepper, add 2 tablespoons water and knead together by hand to thoroughly combine all of the ingredients.

Cut a lid off the top of the tomatoes and scoop out the seeds and flesh. Fill the tomato cases with the mince mixture, replace their lids and place in a baking dish. Drizzle with the olive oil and cook in the preheated oven for 20 minutes.

Suggestion

Serve these stuffed tomatoes with potato purée (p. 254) and drizzled with some of the cooking juices.

HAMBURGERS WITH ONION JAM

Makes 4

700 g (1 lb 9 oz) minced (ground) beef

8 tablespoons onion jam

200 g (7 oz) rocket (arugula)

2 tablespoons olive oil

60 g (2¼ oz) butter

4 eggs

4 bread rolls

4 tablespoons mayonnaise

4 tablespoons tomato sauce (ketchup)

Special equipment
Wooden skewers

Preparation time
20 minutes

Cooking time
25 minutes

Combine the minced meat with half the onion jam in a medium bowl and season with salt and pepper. Make 4 patties of equal size. Wash and dry the rocket.

Heat the olive oil in a large frying pan over medium–high heat. Add the burgers and cook for 2 minutes on each side, so they stay quite rare. Transfer to a plate. Add the butter to the pan and carefully crack in the eggs. Cook to your liking and season with salt and pepper. Transfer to a plate and set aside.

Preheat the oven to 170°C (325°F). Halve the rolls and toast them under the griller (broiler). Brush the bottom halves with mayonnaise, divide the rocket between them and place the burgers on top. Spoon on some onion jam, then place the eggs and tomato sauce on top. Top with the other half of the rolls and secure with a wooden skewer (being careful not to pierce the egg yolk). Warm the burgers in the oven for 2 minutes.

Suggestion
Serve with potato crisps (p. 242).

BRAISED BEEF WITH SAGE

Serves 6

1 head garlic

4 tablespoons olive oil

1.4 kg (3 lb 2 oz) stewing beef (blade, chuck or shin), cut into large cubes

2 tablespoons plain (all-purpose) flour

1.5 litres (52 fl oz/6 cups) red wine

1 sprig thyme

2 bay leaves

2 sprigs sage

Special equipment
Large casserole dish (with lid)

Preparation time
25 minutes

Cooking time
2 hours 30 minutes

Peel the garlic cloves and remove the sprout inside.

Heat the oil in a large casserole dish over high heat. Season the meat with salt and pepper and cook in batches until well browned on all sides. Reduce the heat to medium, add the flour and cook for 2 minutes, stirring. Blend in the wine and add the thyme, bay leaves and garlic cloves.

Pour in 500 ml (17 fl oz/2 cups) water. Stir through, cover and reduce the heat to very low. Simmer for 2 hours 30 minutes, adding a little water if the sauce reduces too much.

Thirty minutes before the end of the cooking time, add the sprigs of sage so they gently infuse the sauce. Prick the meat to check for doneness (it should be very tender).

Mash the garlic cloves into the sauce, season with salt and pepper and serve from the dish at the table.

STRIPLOIN STEAK WITH BAY LEAF AND CURRY OIL

..., about
... g/1 lb 9 oz)

100 ml (3½ fl oz) olive oil

1 teaspoon turmeric

1 tablespoon
curry powder

4 bay leaves

Preparation time
15 minutes

Cooking time
6 minutes

Cut the meat into thick pieces and season with salt and pepper. Heat 2 tablespoons of the oil in a large frying pan over medium–high heat. Add the beef and cook for 3–5 minutes each side (3 minutes each side for rare). Transfer to a plate.

Add the remaining oil, turmeric, curry powder and bay leaves to the cooking juices in the pan and cook for 1–2 minutes, stirring with a spatula. Pour this sauce over the meat and serve.

Suggestion
Serve with potato purée (p. 254).

MEATBALLS WITH BASIL IN GAZPACHO

Serves 4

1 large handful basil

700 g (1 lb 9 oz) minced (ground) beef

1 onion

1 large cucumber

800 g (1 lb 12 oz) whole peeled tomatoes

50 ml (1½ fl oz) olive oil, plus 2 tablespoons extra

1 teaspoon Tabasco sauce

2 tablespoons sherry vinegar

Special equipment
Food processor

Preparation time
25 minutes

Resting time (gazpacho)
1 hour

Cooking time
10 minutes

Wash and chop the basil leaves. Combine the basil with the minced meat in a large bowl and season with salt and pepper. Make meatballs of equal size. Cover and set them aside in the refrigerator for 1 hour.

To make the gazpacho, peel and dice the onion. Peel and seed the cucumber. Blend together the peeled tomatoes with their juice, the 50 ml (1½ fl oz) of olive oil, cucumber, onion, Tabasco and vinegar in the food processor. Adjust the seasoning and set aside in the refrigerator for 1 hour.

Heat the extra olive oil in a large frying pan over medium–high heat. Cook the meatballs for 5 minutes (the meat should stay raw in the centre of the meatballs).

Pour the chilled gazpacho into deep dishes, add the hot meatballs and serve.

BEEF STEW WITH OLIVES AND BACON

Serves 4

2 onions

4 garlic cloves

700 g (1 lb 9 oz) bull
stewing beef (or regular
stewing beef such as
blade, chuck or shin),
cut into large cubes

750 ml (26 fl oz/3 cups)
red wine

100 ml (3½ fl oz) olive oil

2 bay leaves

5 sprigs thyme

3 rashers bacon
or 3 slices speck

200 g (7 oz) black
olives, pitted

Preparation time
45 minutes

Resting time
24 hours

Cooking time
2 hours 30 minutes

Peel and chop the onions. Bruise the garlic cloves in their skin.

Put the meat in a large bowl. Combine the wine, half the olive oil, the bay leaves, thyme, onion and garlic, and pour over the beef. Mix to combine, cover and marinate in the refrigerator for 24 hours.

On the day you are serving the dish, chop the bacon into chunks. Heat the remaining olive oil in a large cast-iron casserole dish over high heat. Add the bacon and cook for 1–2 minutes. Add the olives, meat and marinade. Stir to combine, reduce the heat to low and simmer for 2 hours 30 minutes, stirring occasionally, until the meat is cooked and tender. Season to taste and serve.

Suggestion
Serve hot with potato purée (p. 254).

HAMBURGERS WITH WASHED RIND CHEESE

Makes 4

800 g (1 lb 12 oz) minced (ground) beef

2 tablespoons dijon mustard

100 g (3½ oz) dandelion greens (or curly endive, frisée lettuce or radicchio)

4 tablespoons wholegrain mustard

2 tablespoons mayonnaise

4 very thin slices prosciutto-style (dry-cured) or mountain ham

4 hamburger buns

1 tablespoon sunflower oil

4 thick slices washed rind cheese (such as Taleggio, Epoisses or Pont-l'Evêque)

2 tablespoons walnut oil

Preparation time
25 minutes

Cooking time
10 minutes

Put the minced beef in a large bowl and season with salt and pepper. Add the dijon mustard and combine vigorously by hand. Shape into 4 patties of equal size. Cover and place in the refrigerator for 25 minutes.

Preheat the oven to 180°C (350°F). Wash and dry the dandelion greens. Combine the wholegrain mustard with the mayonnaise. Crisp the ham in a dry frying pan and set it aside (you can fold the slices in two or cut them into several pieces). Cut the buns in half and warm them in the oven for 2–3 minutes.

A little before serving time, heat the sunflower oil in a large frying pan over medium–high heat or preheat the barbecue. Cook the burgers for 2 minutes on each side, or to your taste. Spread the bottom half of the buns with the mustard mayonnaise, place the burgers on top and add the slices of ham and cheese. Place on a baking tray and warm in the oven for 10 minutes to melt the cheese.

Dress the dandelion greens with the walnut oil.

Remove the burgers from the oven, top with the dandelion greens and the other bun halves. Press down gently on the hamburgers to keep the filling in place and serve.

BEEF CHEEKS BRAISED IN RED WINE

Serves 6

4 French shallots

2 garlic cloves

50 g (1¾ oz) butter

2 tablespoons
sunflower oil

4 beef cheeks

1 large sprig thyme

1 bay leaf

1 tablespoon plain
(all-purpose) flour

750 ml (26 fl oz/3 cups)
red wine

500 ml (17 fl oz/2 cups)
beef broth or
brown veal stock

Preparation time
35 minutes

Cooking time
2 hours 15 minutes

Peel and chop the shallots and garlic.

Heat the butter and oil in a casserole dish over medium–high heat. Season the beef cheeks with salt and pepper. Cook for 2–3 minutes on each side, or until well browned. Add the shallots and garlic, thyme and bay leaf and cook for 2–3 minutes. Add the flour and blend in the red wine. Reduce the heat to medium–low and cook until the liquid is reduced by half.

Add the broth or stock and 400 m (14 fl oz) water. Simmer for 2 hours, stirring occasionally, or until the beef is soft and meltingly tender.

Season to taste and serve from the casserole dish at the table.

Suggestion
Serve with potato purée (p. 254).

RIB STEAK WITH CRISPY ONIONS

Serves 4–5

1 large rib steak (about 1.4 kg/3 lb 2 oz)

2 tablespoons sunflower oil

50 g (1¾ oz) butter

2 large onions

2 tablespoons plain (all-purpose) flour

Oil for deep-frying

Special equipment
Deep-fryer (or large saucepan)

Preparation time
20 minutes

Cooking time
15 minutes

Preheat the oven to 180°C (350°F).

Season the steak with salt and pepper. Heat the sunflower oil in a large frying pan over medium–high heat. Cook the steak for 2 minutes on each side, then transfer to a large baking tray.

Brush the steak with the butter and cook in the preheated oven for 10 minutes, or longer if you prefer a well-done steak. When cooked to your liking, remove the meat from the oven, cover with foil and let it rest for 5 minutes, turning at least once.

Meanwhile, peel and slice the onions and coat with the flour. Heat the oil to 160°C (315°F), or when a cube of bread turns golden brown in 30–35 seconds, and deep-fry the onions for 1–2 minutes, or until golden and crispy. Drain on paper towel.

Cut the rib steak into thick slices and place on individual plates. Spoon over the cooking and meat juices and scatter over the deep-fried onions.

Suggestion
Sautéed potatoes with olives and basil (p. 282) or potato purée (p. 254) would be perfect with this dish.

BRAISED BEEF WITH MUSHROOMS AND THYME

Serves 4

4 garlic cloves

120 ml (3¾ fl oz) sunflower oil

1.2 kg (2 lb 11 oz) stewing beef (blade, chuck or shin), cut into large cubes

100 ml (3½ fl oz) red or white wine vinegar

2 tablespoons plain (all-purpose) flour

1 litre (35 fl oz/4 cups) good red wine

2 sprigs thyme

4 bay leaves

1 kg (2 lb 4 oz) fresh cep (porchini) mushrooms (or reconstituted dried ceps or other fresh mushrooms of choice), washed and scraped

Special equipment
Cast-iron casserole dish

Preparation time
35 minutes

Cooking time
3 hours

Peel and crush the garlic cloves.

Heat 4 tablespoons of the oil in a large cast-iron casserole dish over medium–high heat. Add the meat and cook for 2–3 minutes, until browned on all sides. Add 4 tablespoons of the wine vinegar and boil, stirring, to deglaze the pan.

Add the flour and cook, stirring, for 2–3 minutes. Blend in the red wine and 250 ml (9 fl oz/1 cup) water. Add half the thyme and bay leaves. Reduce the heat to low and gently simmer for at least 3 hours, stirring occasionally.

Ten minutes before serving time, heat the remaining oil in a large frying pan over medium–high heat. Cook the mushrooms for 2–3 minutes then add the remaining thyme and bay leaves. Once the mushrooms start to brown, add the garlic and the remaining wine vinegar. Cook until the liquid is reduced by half. Season with salt and pepper and remove from the heat.

Serve the meat with the vinegar sauce and the mushrooms.

GOULASH

Serves 4

6 tomatoes

2 red capsicums (peppers)

3 large onions

50 g (1¾ oz) butter

3 tablespoons
sunflower oil

1.2 kg (2 lb 11 oz)
stewing beef (blade,
chuck or shin),
cut into large cubes

2 sprigs thyme

1 bay leaf

4 tablespoons paprika

1 teaspoon ground cumin

1 tablespoon plain
(all-purpose) flour

100 g (3½ oz) sour cream

Special equipment
Cast-iron casserole dish

Preparation time
25 minutes

Cooking time
2 hours 15 minutes

Seed the tomatoes and chop them into pieces. De-stem the capsicums and slice them into thin strips. Peel and slice the onions.

Heat the butter and oil in a casserole dish over medium–high heat. Season the beef pieces with salt and pepper and cook for 2–3 minutes, or until well browned. Add the thyme and bay leaf, and cook for 1–2 minutes. Add the tomato, capsicum, onion, paprika, cumin and flour. Cook for 2–3 minutes, then add 1.25 litres (44 fl oz/5 cups) water. Reduce the heat to low and simmer for 2 hours, stirring occasionally, or until the meat is cooked and meltingly tender.

Add the sour cream and season with salt and pepper to taste. Stir through and serve immediately.

Suggestion
Serve hot with steamed potatoes or potato purée (p. 254).

BARGEMAN'S BEEF WITH ANCHOVIES

Serves 4

2 carrots

4 garlic cloves

5 French shallots

3 tablespoons peanut oil

1 kg (2 lb 4 oz) stewing beef (blade, chuck or shin, cut into small pieces)

2 sprigs thyme

2 bay leaves

1 tablespoon plain (all-purpose) flour

½ teaspoon tomato paste (concentrated purée)

1.5 litres (52 fl oz/6 cups) red wine

100 g (3½ oz) anchovies in brine

4 slices country-style bread

Special equipment
Cast-iron casserole dish (with lid)

Preparation time
35 minutes

Cooking time
2 hours 30 minutes

Peel the carrots and slice into rounds. Bruise 3 of the garlic cloves in their skin. Peel and slice the shallots.

Heat the oil and sauté the garlic cloves and shallots in a cast-iron casserole dish over medium–high heat. Add the beef and cook for 2–3 minutes, or until browned on all sides. Add the carrot, thyme and bay leaves and stir to combine. Add the flour and tomato paste and stir to combine. Season with pepper, stir, and reduce the heat to low. Add the wine and 250 ml (9 fl oz/1 cup) water and stir gently to combine. Cover and simmer for 2 hours 30 minutes, stirring occasionally. (Add a little water if the liquid reduces too much.)

Rinse the anchovy fillets under cold water. Toast the bread and rub with the remaining garlic clove.

When the meat is meltingly tender and the sauce is smooth and thick, remove from the heat. Set aside 4 anchovy fillets to garnish and crush the others into the sauce with a fork.

Arrange the meat, carrots and shallots on the toast in deep plates, pour the sauce over and garnish with the anchovy fillets. Serve hot.

BEEF AND ONION STIR-FRY

Serves 4

400 g (14 oz) lean and tender beef for pan-frying (inside round, rump, tenderloin, striploin)

1 large carrot

2 large onions

4 tablespoons peanut oil

1 teaspoon caster (superfine) sugar

2 tablespoons satay sauce

3 tablespoons Chinese-style soy sauce

1 tablespoon oyster sauce

50 ml (1½ fl oz) beef broth (left over from a pot-au-feu or bouillon made from a stock cube)

1 teaspoon cornflour (cornstarch)

Special equipment
Mandoline
(or large sharp knife)

Wok

Preparation time
20 minutes

Cooking time
15 minutes

Cut the meat into thin slices. Peel and slice the carrot thinly using a mandoline. Peel and slice the onions.

Heat the oil in a wok over high heat. Add the onions and carrots and stir-fry for 1–2 minutes. Add the sugar and continue to stir-fry for 5 minutes. Add the meat and cook for 2 minutes. Add the satay sauce, soy sauce and oyster sauce and cook, stirring, for 1 minute to deglaze the wok. Blend the cornflour into the beef broth and add to the wok. Stir through and cook for a further 5 minutes. Serve immediately with steamed Asian greens.

RIB EYE STEAK WITH GARLIC CHIPS

Serves 4

6 garlic cloves

100 ml (3½ fl oz) olive oil

60 g (2¼ oz) butter

4 large rib eye steaks
(about 200 g/7 oz each)

1 tablespoon dried thyme
or oregano

Special equipment
Sharp knife

Preparation time
35 minutes

Cooking time
20 minutes

Peel the garlic cloves, remove the sprouts in the middle and cut into thin slivers using a sharp knife.

Heat the oil in a large frying pan over high heat. Cook the garlic slivers for 1–2 minutes, until golden brown. Transfer to a plate lined with paper towel. Strain the oil and return it to the heat in a clean frying pan. Season the steaks with salt and pepper. Cook for 2–3 minutes on each side. Transfer to serving plates.

Add the garlic chips and thyme to the pan. Stir to combine and remove from the heat. Spoon over the steaks and serve immediately.

Suggestion
Serve these rib eye steaks with crispy potato chips (p. 238).

BEEF STIR-FRY WITH ROASTED PEANUTS

Serves 4

800 g (1 lb 12 oz)
rump steak

4 garlic cloves

1 large handful
coriander (cilantro)

200 g (7 oz) roasted
salted peanuts

2 tablespoons peanut oil

100 ml (3½ fl oz)
coconut milk

Special equipment
A sharp knife

Mortar and pestle

Preparation time
20 minutes

Cooking time
5 minutes

Cut the rump steak into thin slivers. Peel and chop the garlic. Wash and chop the coriander, including the stems. Roughly crush the peanuts in a mortar.

Heat the oil in a large frying pan over high heat. Add the crushed peanuts and cook for 1–2 minutes. Add the steak and garlic, season with salt and pepper and stir-fry for 5 minutes. Add the coconut milk and boil, stirring, for 30 seconds to deglaze the pan. Remove the pan from the heat and toss the coriander through.

TENDER BEEF WITH TOMATOES AND CORIANDER

Serves 4

800 g (1 lb 12 oz) inside round (topside) or rump steak

1 handful coriander (cilantro)

4 garlic cloves

3 French shallots

120 ml (3¾ fl oz) olive oil

250 g (9 oz) cherry tomatoes

3 tablespoons soy sauce

Special equipment
A sharp knife

Preparation time
20 minutes

Cooking time
15 minutes

Cut the meat into small slices about 5 cm (2 inches) across. Remove and wash the coriander leaves and set aside. Peel and chop the garlic. Peel and finely slice the shallots.

Heat half the olive oil in a large frying pan over medium–high heat. Add the garlic and cook for 1 minute. Add the cherry tomatoes and cook until they start to soften but are not splitting. Transfer the garlic and tomatoes to a large plate.

Wipe out the frying pan with paper towel. Heat the remaining olive over high heat and cook the beef for 2 minutes on each side, so the meat remains quite rare.

Add the soy sauce and boil, stirring, for 30 seconds to deglaze the pan. Season with salt and pepper, return the garlic and tomatoes to the pan, and cook for 2 minutes, stirring gently. Remove from the heat. Add the reserved coriander, stir through and serve immediately.

Suggestion
Serve this dish with potato purée (see p. 254) or steamed potatoes.

POTATOES

POTATOES

Potatoes, yes, but which ones? You don't make mash, chips, steamed potatoes, sautéed potatoes, potato crisps and soufflé potatoes with the same potato. It's important to distinguish between a waxy potato – such as Dutch cream and kipfler – and a floury/starchy potato – such as king edward, coliban, russet and idaho. Should you choose a late potato or a new potato? Now it's getting complicated. Confused? You don't need a university degree to cook potatoes well, but there's a minimum you need to know. Here are a few broad rules: for chips, mashes and soups, choose floury/starchy potatoes. For stews or baked dishes, use all-purpose potatoes (such as red pontiac, sebago, kennebec, desiree and yukon gold) which will absorb the flavours of the other ingredients. For a potato salad or sautéed potatoes, use waxy varieties, which stay firm when cooked. New potatoes are full of water – they are fresh vegetables, just like beans or peas – so they don't keep for more than a week. There's no need to peel them – a quick scrub does the job. Those are the few broad rules to start with, and here are more than a few recipes to follow and hoe into.

CRISPY POTATO CHIPS

Serves 4–6

1 kg (2 lb 4 oz) large
floury/starchy potatoes

Oil for deep-frying

Special equipment

Tea towel (dish towel)

Preparation time

35 minutes

Cooking time

20 minutes

Peel and wash the potatoes, then cut them into large, regular chips. Wash the chips in cold water and dry them well in a large tea towel (dish towel). Heat the oil to 160°C (315°F) in a deep-fryer or large saucepan (it is ready when a cube of bread turns golden brown in 30–35 seconds). Cook the chips for 7–8 minutes in two batches, if necessary, to prevent them from sticking to each other. Set the chips aside to cool completely.

At serving time, cook the chips a second time in 190°C (375°) oil (ready when a cube of bread turns golden brown in 10 seconds) for 4–5 minutes, stirring occasionally, or until they are crispy and golden brown. Remove and drain the the chips, season with salt and serve immediately, plain or with mayonnaise or tomato sauce (ketchup), on their own or as a side for grilled meats – or one of the many dishes suggested in this book!

NEW POTATOES IN THEIR SKIN WITH SAGE BUTTER

Serves 4

1 kg (2 lb 4 oz) small
new potatoes

2 tablespoons olive oil

100 g (3½ oz) butter

10 sage leaves

Special equipment
Tea towel (dish towel)

Preparation time
10 minutes

Cooking time
45 minutes

Preheat the oven to 180°C (350°F). Scrub the potatoes in their skin under cold running water, then dry them in a tea towel (dish towel). Arrange them in a large roasting tin and drizzle with the olive oil. Cook in the preheated oven, turning occasionally, for 40 minutes or until golden brown.

Meanwhile, melt the butter in a small saucepan over low heat. Add the sage leaves and cook until they are crisp. Remove from the heat (the butter should be slightly brown). Set aside at room temperature.

Once the potatoes are cooked, transfer them to a large frying pan over medium heat. Add the sage leaves and butter. Heat through, tossing gently, for 2–3 minutes and serve with a salad or as a side to roast beef or chicken.

POTATO CRISPS

Serves 4

1 kg (2 lb 4 oz) boiling (waxy) potatoes

Oil for deep-frying

Special equipment

Large tea towel
(dish towel)

Mandoline
(or large sharp knife)

Preparation time
15 minutes

Cooking time
10 minutes

Peel and rinse the potatoes. Using a mandoline, cut them into thin slices, 2 mm ($^1/_{16}$ inch) thick. Rinse the potato slices in a large quantity of cold water, then drain and dry them in a large tea towel (dish towel).

Put enough oil for deep-frying in a deep-fryer or large saucepan. Heat to 180°C (350°F) (ready when a cube of bread turns golden brown in 15 seconds) and cook the potato slices in small batches for 3–4 minutes, or until they are golden and crispy. Drain on paper towel, season with salt and let the potato crisps cool before serving.

AMANDINE POTATOES

Serves 4–6

1 kg (2 lb 4 oz) large bintje (yellow finn) or similar potatoes

40 g (1½ oz) butter

110 g (3¾ oz) almond meal

2 egg yolks

2 whole eggs

200 g (7 oz) plain (all-purpose) flour

100 g (3½ oz) breadcrumbs

Oil for deep-frying

Special equipment
Potato masher

Wooden toothpicks

Preparation time
45 minutes

Resting time
1 hour 30 minutes

Cooking time
40 minutes

Peel the potatoes and cut them into large pieces. Put them in a large saucepan of salted water over high heat and bring to the boil. Reduce the heat to low and cook for 30 minutes.

Drain the potatoes, transfer to a medium bowl and mash using a potato masher. Add the butter and half of the almond meal. Let the mixture cool for 5 minutes.

Mix the mashed potato with a wooden spatula. Keep mixing as you add the egg yolks one at a time, until you have a thick mash. Season with salt and pepper, cover with plastic wrap and set aside for 1 hour in the refrigerator.

Flour your hands and roll the cold mashed potato mixture into pear shapes, then insert a toothpick or a piece of spaghetti in the top to handle them more easily. Place them on a large plate and set aside for 30 minutes in the refrigerator.

Crack the whole eggs into a shallow bowl and whisk lightly. Put the flour on a large plate. Mix the remaining almond meal with the breadcrumbs and put on another large plate. Roll the potato 'pears' in the flour, then in the egg mixture and in the breadcrumbs to finish.

Put enough oil for deep-frying in a deep-fryer or large saucepan. Heat to 180°C (350°F) (ready when a cube of bread turns golden brown in 15 seconds) and cook the potato 'pears' for 2–3 minutes, or until golden. Drain on paper towel, season with salt and pepper and serve as a side to a fine rib or other steak.

CHEESY POTATO PURÉE

Serves 4–6

1 garlic clove (optional)

400 g (14 oz) tomme cheese (aligot, poutine or similar semi-soft cheese)

1.2 kg (2 lb 11 oz) floury/starchy or mashing potatoes

450 ml (16 fl oz) crème fraîche

Special equipment
Food mill

Preparation time
35 minutes

Cooking time
40 minutes

Peel and chop the garlic, if using. Make shavings of the cheese.

Peel the potatoes and cut them into large pieces. Put them in a large saucepan with plenty of salted water over high heat and bring to the boil. Reduce the heat to low and cook for 30 minutes.

Drain the potatoes and put them through a food mill. Transfer the potato purée to a large saucepan over low heat. Add a little of the cooking water and the garlic, if using, and incorporate the crème fraîche, then the cheese, little by little, stirring vigorously with a spatula. The cheese should be melted and the purée should be smooth and flowing. Serve hot with grilled beef.

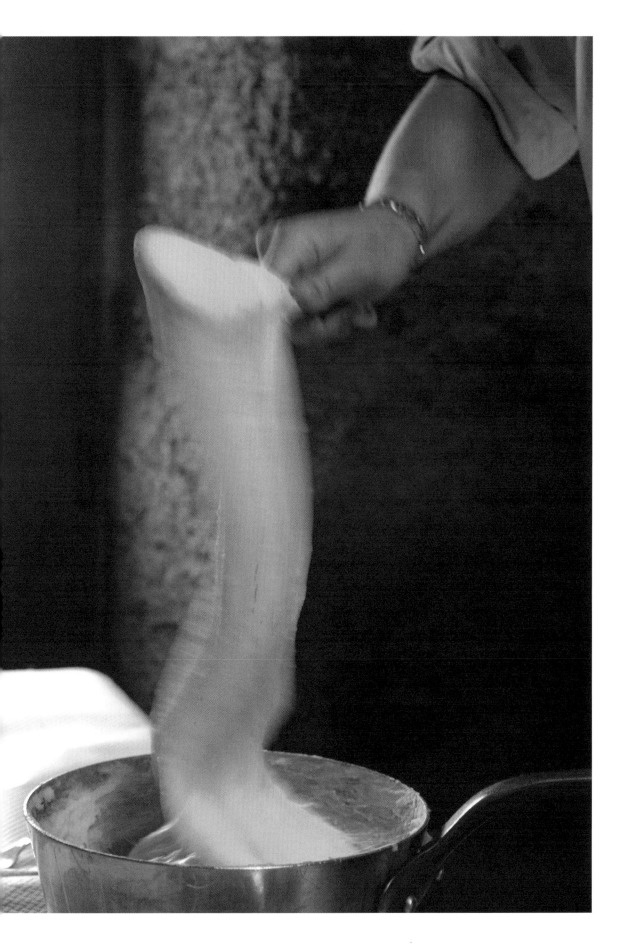

SOUFFLÉ POTATOES

Serves 4

500 g (1 lb 2 oz) large boiling (waxy) potatoes

Peanut oil for deep-frying

Special equipment

Mandoline
(or large sharp knife)

Large tea towel
(dish towel)

Preparation time

30 minutes

Cooking time

10 minutes

Peel the potatoes. Trim the rounded ends and sides of the potatoes to make uniformly shaped rectangular blocks. Cut 5 mm (¼ inch) thick slices lengthways using a mandoline or a very sharp knife (the potatoes won't puff up if the slices aren't evenly sized). Rinse the slices of potato in cold water and dry them well with a tea towel (dish towel).

Put enough peanut oil for deep-frying in a deep-fryer or large saucepan. Heat to 140°C (275°F) (ready when a cube of bread turns golden brown in 40 seconds) and deep-fry the potato slices for 5 minutes. Drain on paper towel and set aside to cool completely.

Reheat the oil to 160°C (315°F) (ready when a cube of bread turns golden brown in 30–35 seconds) and deep-fry the potato slices again in several batches (they will puff up) and drain on paper towel.

At serving time, deep-fry the potato slices (now puffs) one last time, all at once, at 180°C (350°F) (ready when a cube of bread turns golden brown in 15 seconds), until golden. Drain on paper towel and serve very hot, to accompany grilled or braised meat.

POTATOES AND APPLES SAUTÉED IN GOOSE FAT

Serves 4

500 g (1 lb 2 oz) boiling (waxy) potatoes

500 g (1 lb 2 oz) golden delicious apples

3 tablespoons sunflower oil

3 tablespoons goose fat (or duck fat)

Preparation time
20 minutes

Cooking time
35 minutes

Peel the potatoes and cut into chunks. Peel, core and cut the apples into pieces the same size as the potatoes.

Heat the oil in a large frying pan over medium–high heat. Add the potatoes, reduce the heat to low, and cook for 15 minutes. Add the apples and goose fat, increase the heat to medium and cook, stirring often, for 15–20 minutes, or until the potatoes and apples are cooked and golden brown (insert the tip of a knife into the potatoes to check they are cooked). Season with salt and pepper and serve as a side for a bavette (flank) or hanger steak.

POTATO PURÉE

Serves 4–6

1 kg (2 lb 4 oz)
floury/starchy or
mashing potatoes

250 ml (9 fl oz/1 cup)
full-cream milk

50 ml (1½ fl oz)
crème fraîche

150 g (5½ oz) cold butter

Special equipment
Food mill

Preparation time
35 minutes

Cooking time
45 minutes

Peel the potatoes and cut them into large pieces. Put them in a large saucepan with plenty of salted water over high heat and bring to the boil. Reduce the heat to low and cook for 20-25 minutes, depending on their size.

When the potatoes are cooked, mix the milk and crème fraîche together. Cut the cold butter into small pieces.

Drain the potatoes and put them through the food mill, adding the milk mixture little by little, and half of the cold butter pieces. Season with salt, then mix with a wooden spatula while gradually adding the remaining butter. Serve hot with a saucy beef dish, beef skewers or pan-fried steak.

POTATO AND BASIL FRITTERS

Serves 4

1 large handful basil

2 garlic cloves

1 pinch chilli powder

200 g (7 oz) potato purée (p. 254)

200 g (7 oz) plain (all-purpose) flour

11 g (¼ oz/2 teaspoons) baking powder

Oil for deep-frying

Special equipment
Garlic crusher

Preparation time
25 minutes

Resting time
Overnight

Cooking time
20 minutes

Wash and chop the basil leaves. Crush the garlic cloves and combine with the chilli powder.

Put the potato purée, flour and 100 ml (3½ fl oz) lukewarm water in a medium bowl and whisk to make a smooth, homogenous batter. Add the baking powder, basil, and garlic and chilli powder. Season with salt and pepper and stir to combine. Cover and put in the refrigerator to set overnight.

At serving time, put enough oil for deep-frying in a deep-fryer or large saucepan. Heat to 180°C (350°F) (ready when a cube of bread turns golden brown in 15 seconds). Using a large spoon, drop small quantities of batter into the hot oil and and cook until the fritters are golden brown. Drain on paper towel, season with salt and pepper and serve very hot with drinks or as a side to grilled meat.

POTATO-STUFFED TOMATOES

Serves 4

4 large floury/starchy or mashing potatoes

8 garlic cloves

2 sprigs thyme

2 bay leaves

250 ml (9 fl oz/1 cup) milk

4 tablespoons olive oil

1 teaspoon mixed dried herbs

4 large oxheart tomatoes, or other large tomatoes

Special equipment
Food mill with
a fine blade

Preparation time
30 minutes

Cooking time
40 minutes

Peel the potatoes and cook them in a saucepan of salted water – they should be very well cooked. Drain and set them aside on a plate. Peel the potatoes, put them in a large saucepan with plenty of salted water over high heat and bring to the boil. Reduce the heat to low and cook for 20-25 minutes, or until well cooked.

Peel and chop the garlic cloves. Put in a small saucepan with the thyme, bay leaf and milk over medium–low heat. Heat gently to infuse the milk. Strain the milk, reserving the garlic cloves. Set aside.

Cut the potatoes and put them through the food mill, adding the lukewarm milk and the cooked garlic cloves, to make a smooth purée. Add 2 tablespoons of the olive oil and the mixed herbs and season with salt and pepper. Mix gently and set aside.

Preheat the oven to 180°C (350°F). Cut a lid off the top of each tomato, scoop out the pulp (you can use it for another recipe) and fill the shells with the potato purée.

Replace the lids and arrange the tomatoes in a large ovenproof dish. Drizzle with the remaining olive oil and cook in the preheated oven for 20 minutes. Don't overcook the tomatoes or they will collapse.

Suggestion
Serve hot or warm with a rocket salad.

HERB AND POTATO PANCAKES

Serves 4

1 small handful
flat-leaf parsley

5 sprigs mint

1 small handful
coriander (cilantro)

1 small handful chives

100 g (3½ oz) baby
spinach leaves

2 garlic cloves

600 g (1 lb 5 oz) potato
purée (p. 254)

2 eggs, lightly whisked

50 ml (1½ fl oz) thin
(pouring) cream

40 g (1½ oz) plain
(all-purpose) flour

100 ml (3½ fl oz) olive oil

Special equipment
Food processor

Preparation time
40 minutes

Cooking time
25 minutes

Wash and chop the parsley, mint and coriander leaves. Wash and chop the chives. Wash the baby spinach leaves. Peel and crush the garlic. Drop the parsley, mint, coriander and baby spinach into a saucepan of boiling water for 30 seconds. Drain, squeeze gently and process with the garlic in a food processor.

Warm the potato purée in a microwave oven to soften it. Make a hollow in the middle and add the eggs, cream and flour. Whisk to make a smooth batter. Season with salt and pepper and add the puréed herbs and the chives.

Heat the oil in a large frying pan over medium–high heat. Pour in a large spoonful of the batter for each pancake. Cook for 2–3 minutes on each side and transfer to a plate lined with paper towel. Serve the pancakes immediately either on their own, with a salad or as a side to grilled meats.

FRIED POTATOES WITH AÏOLI

Serves 4

600 g (1 lb 5 oz) large waxy (boiling) potatoes

Oil for deep-frying

For the aïoli

5 pink garlic cloves (or white if not available)

1 egg yolk (optional)

100 ml (3½ fl oz) olive oil

1 tablespoon milk

Special equipment
Mortar and pestle

Preparation time
30 minutes

Cooking time
10 minutes

To make the aïoli, peel the garlic cloves and remove the sprouts in the middle. Pound the garlic in the mortar and season with salt and pepper. Add the egg yolk, if using (it will make it easier to emulsify the aioli) and pour in the oil, little by little, mixing at the same time, to emulsify the aioli. Add the milk and mix to combine. Set aside at room temperature.

Peel and wash the potatoes. Cut them into evenly sized cubes. Heat enough oil for deep-frying in a deep-fryer or large saucepan over high heat to 170°C (325°F), or when a cube of bread turns golden brown in 20 seconds. Deep-fry the potato cubes in batches until golden brown. Drain on paper towel. Set aside and keep warm.

Serve the fried potatoes on a large dish with aïoli spooned over and seasoned with salt and pepper.

POTATO AND QUINOA CROQUETTES

Serves 4

600 g (1 lb 5 oz) potato purée (p. 254)

3 eggs, lightly whisked

50 ml (1½ fl oz) thin (pouring) cream

60 g (2¼ oz) plain (all-purpose) flour

200 g (7 oz) cooked quinoa

120 ml (3¾ fl oz) sunflower oil

Preparation time
40 minutes

Cooking time
20 minutes

Warm the purée in a microwave oven a little to soften it. Make a hollow in the middle and add the eggs, cream and flour. Whisk to make a smooth batter. Season with salt and pepper, add the quinoa and mix to combine.

Heat the oil in a large frying pan over medium–high heat. Pour in large spoonfuls of purée mixture for each croquette. Cook for 2–3 minutes on each side and transfer to a plate lined with paper towel. Serve the croquettes immediately on their own, with a salad or as a side to grilled meats.

POTATO AND TURMERIC FRITTERS

Serves 4–6

2 handfuls
coriander (cilantro)

4 garlic cloves

500 g (1 lb 2 oz) large
floury/starchy potatoes

1 tablespoon turmeric

1 egg, lightly whisked

1 teaspoon chilli powder

200 g (7 oz) plain
(all-purpose) flour

Oil for deep-frying

Preparation time
1 hour

Resting time
30 minutes

Cooking time
10–12 minutes

Wash and chop the coriander leaves. Peel and chop the garlic.

Peel the potatoes and cut them into large pieces. Put them in a large saucepan of salted water over high heat and bring to the boil. Reduce the heat to low and cook for 30 minutes. Drain and mash in a medium bowl, allow to cool a little and add the turmeric, coriander, garlic, egg and chilli. Season with salt and pepper and combine.

Whisk the flour and 150 ml (5 fl oz) water in a mixing bowl and set aside in the refrigerator.

Make balls of potato the size of a small egg, place them on a large tray and let them dry out for 30 minutes in the refrigerator.

Heat enough oil for deep-frying in a deep-fryer or large saucepan over high heat to 170°C (325°F) or when a cube of bread turns golden brown in 20 seconds. Dip the balls, three at a time, in the batter, and deep-fry for 3–4 minutes, moving them around. Drain on paper towel and serve the fritters immediately with a salad or as a side to grilled meats.

CREAMY POTATO GRATIN

Serves 4–6

3 garlic cloves

2 kg (4 lb 8 oz) large all-purpose potatoes

500 ml (17 fl oz/2 cups) thin (pouring) cream

1 pinch ground nutmeg

2 tablespoons crème fraîche

Special equipment
Mandoline
(or large sharp knife)

Preparation time
30 minutes

Cooking time
45 minutes

Preheat the oven to 170°C (325°F). Peel and thinly slice the garlic cloves. Peel the potatoes, then slice them thinly using a mandoline (or a large sharp knife).

Place the potato slices in a large baking dish or tin (do not rinse them) and pour the cream over. Add the garlic and nutmeg, season with salt and pepper, toss together the ingredients and pack the potato down well in the dish. Top with the crème fraîche, season with salt and pepper again and cook in the preheated oven for 45 minutes, or until cooked through (check by inserting the tip of a knife) and golden brown on top.

Serve as a main course with a green salad or as a side to a roast.

TORTILLA

Serves 4

3 large onions

1 kg (2 lb 4 oz) waxy (boiling) potatoes

5 eggs

1 pinch chilli powder

100 ml (3½ fl oz) olive oil

180 g (6¼ oz) butter

Preparation time
15 minutes

Cooking time
1 hour

Peel and slice the onions. Peel the potatoes, cut into small chunks and wash and dry them. Whisk the eggs in a medium bowl, then add the chilli powder and season with salt and pepper.

Heat 4 tablespoons of the olive oil in a heavy-based frying pan over medium heat. Add the potatoes and cook, stirring and without browning too much, for 15 minutes. Add the onions, toss gently to combine, reduce the heat to low and cook for a further 25 minutes, stirring occasionally.

Add the potatoes and onions to the bowl with the eggs and mix together gently. Add the butter and the remaining olive oil to the frying pan. Pour the egg mixture into the pan and spread evenly over the whole surface. Reduce the heat to low and cook the tortilla for 10 minutes without stirring (you can add a little more oil if it is sticking to the sides).

Once the bottom is well cooked, gently flip the tortilla over using a plate and cook the other side for 8 minutes, still over low heat.

Turn the tortilla onto a large serving plate, let it cool a little and serve with a green salad.

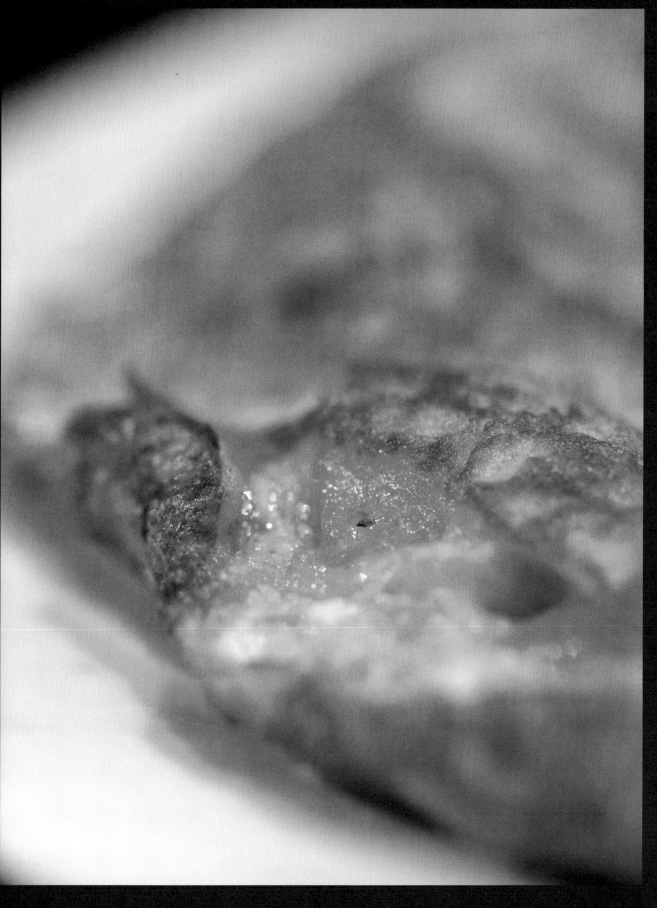

SHOESTRING POTATOES WITH GARLIC AND PARSLEY

Serves 4

1 handful flat-leaf parsley

5 garlic cloves

1 kg (2 lb 4 oz) all-purpose potatoes

Oil for deep-frying

Special equipment

Mandoline
(or large sharp knife)

Spider strainer

Tea towel
(dish towel)

Preparation time
40 minutes

Cooking time
5 minutes

Wash, dry and chop the parsley leaves. Peel and chop the garlic. Peel and wash the potatoes. Cut them into thin slices, then into matchsticks, using a mandoline. Dry the potato in a large clean tea towel (dish towel).

Heat enough oil for deep-frying in a deep-fryer or large saucepan over high heat to 180°C (350°F), or when a cube of bread turns golden brown in 20 seconds. Deep-fry the potato in several batches, stirring with a spider strainer so it doesn't stick together, until golden. Drain on paper towel and transfer to a large serving dish. Season with salt and add the parsley and garlic. Toss and serve immediately.

POTATO PURÉE WITH TRUFFLES

Serves 4–6

1 pink garlic clove (or white if not available)

80 g (2¾ oz) butter

1 kg (2 lb 4 oz) old floury/starchy potatoes

250 ml (9 fl oz/1 cup) full-cream milk

1 sprig thyme

160 ml (5¼ fl oz) truffle oil (available from specialty food stores)

25 g (1 oz) truffle slices, in oil

Special equipment
Food mill

Preparation time
35 minutes

Cooking time
30 minutes

Bruise the garlic clove in its skin. Cut the butter into pieces.

Peel the potatoes and cut them into large pieces. Put them in a large saucepan of salted water over high heat and bring to the boil. Reduce the heat to low and cook for 30 minutes.

Heat the milk with the thyme and garlic clove in a small saucepan over medium heat. Strain the milk.

Drain the potatoes and put them through a food mill, adding the milk and butter pieces a little at a time. Season with salt and pepper and mix with a wooden spatula, gradually adding the truffle oil.

Warm the truffle slices with their oil gently in a small saucepan over low heat.

Place the potato purée in a large serving dish. Season with salt and pepper and add the truffle slices, with their oil. Serve immediately.

Suggestion

Serve as a side to a saucy beef dish, grilled skewers or a roasted or grilled rib steak.

POTATOES ANNA

Serves 4–6

1 kg (2 lb 4 oz) waxy (boiling) potatoes

150 g (5½ oz) butter, softened at room temperature

1 tablespoon sunflower oil

Special equipment
Mandoline
(or large sharp knife)

8 non-stick tart tins, about 9 cm (3½ inch) diameter (or 1 large tin)

Preparation time
35 minutes

Cooking time
45 minutes

Peel the potatoes and rinse them under cold running water. Dry, then slice into very thin rounds using a mandoline.

Preheat the oven to 180°C (350°F). Grease eight 9 cm (3½ inch) tart tins generously with half the butter. Melt the remaining butter with the olive oil in a small saucepan over medium heat.

Lay the rounds of potato in a circle in the base of the tins, half overlapping them to make a rosette pattern. Season with salt and pepper, brush with a little of the melted butter and oil, then continue to arrange the potatoes around the tin until they reach the top, brushing with the melted butter and oil to finish.

Place the tins on a large baking tray and cook them for 25 minutes in the preheated oven. Remove the baking tray from the oven, carefully turn the potato cakes over, and cook for another 20 minutes, until the tops are golden and crusty.

Unmould the potatoes anna onto a serving dish, season with salt and pepper and serve immediately as a side for a rib steak.

SAUTÉED POTATOES WITH OLIVES AND BASIL

Serves 4–6

1 handful basil

5 garlic cloves

800 g (1 lb 12 oz) small waxy (boiling) potatoes

4 tablespoons olive oil

25 marinated Greek-style olives, pitted

Special equipment

Garlic crusher

Vegetable brush

Preparation time

20 minutes

Cooking time

35 minutes

Rinse, dry and roughly chop the basil leaves.

Peel and crush the garlic cloves. Scrub the potatoes with a brush under lukewarm running water to remove all the dirt. Put them in a large saucepan of salted water over high heat and bring to the boil. Reduce the heat to low and cook for 25 minutes. Drain the potatoes and let them dry for 5 minutes. Cut them in half.

Heat the oil in a large frying pan over medium–high heat. Add the potatoes and cook, tossing, for 5 minutes, or until golden brown. Add the garlic and olives, season with salt and pepper and cook for a further minute. Remove from the heat, add the basil and toss through. Serve immediately as a side for a roast or a rib steak.

CURRY MASHED POTATOES

Serves 4–6

1 kg (2 lb 4 oz) large
floury/starchy potatoes

50 ml (1¾ fl oz) thin
(pouring) cream

2 tablespoons curry
powder

10 curry leaves

100 g (3½ oz) butter

2 tablespoons olive oil

Preparation time
35 minutes

Cooking time
35 minutes

Peel the potatoes, put them in a large saucepan of salted water over high heat and bring to the boil. Reduce the heat to low and cook for 30 minutes.

Meanwhile, heat the cream in a small saucepan with the curry powder and curry leaves over medium–low heat.

Drain the potatoes and mash them with the butter and olive oil. Add the cream mixture to the mashed potato and mix together vigorously. Adjust the seasoning.

Serve hot alongside a roast or grilled steak.

CHIPS AND
SALAD ROLLS

Makes 4

16 lettuce leaves

4 servings crispy potato
chips (p. 238)

4 hot dog buns

3 tablespoons mayonnaise
(preferably home-made)

Preparation time
10 minutes

Cooking time
10 minutes

Wash and dry the lettuce leaves, remove any tough parts, and shred
the lettuce.

Open up the hot dog buns. Combine the lettuce and mayonnaise.
Divide the chips and the dressed lettuce between the hot dog buns
and serve immediately (you can also add a slice of roast beef).

FONDANT POTATOES

Serves 4–6

150 g (5½ oz) butter

1 kg (2 lb 4 oz) medium all-purpose potatoes

500 ml (7 fl oz/2 cups) chicken stock

Special equipment

Large ovenproof dish

Pastry brush

Preparation time

25 minutes

Cooking time

1 hour

Preheat the oven to 170°C (325°F). Cut the butter into pieces and set aside 30 g (1 oz). Peel the potatoes then 'turn' them with a small knife so they are all an identical barrel-like shape.

Arrange the potatoes side by side in a single layer in a large ovenproof dish. Pour in chicken stock to three-quarters up the sides of the potatoes and dot with the 120 g (4½ oz) butter pieces. Season with salt and pepper and cook in the preheated oven for 1 hour, basting the potatoes frequently with the cooking juices so they absorb plenty of stock and butter.

Melt the remaining butter and once the potatoes start to brown brush it over the top. Once the stock has almost completely evaporated, check whether the potatoes are cooked by inserting the tip of a knife (they should be meltingly tender, or 'fondant').

Arrange the potatoes on a serving plate, brush on the remaining melted butter and serve immediately as a side for a beef stew or beef bourguignon.

MOROCCAN POTATO CAKES

Serves 4

4 pink garlic cloves (or white if not available)

1 small handful flat-leaf parsley

2 kg (4 lb 8 oz) all-purpose potatoes

1 teaspoon ground cumin

5 saffron threads

50 g (1¾ oz) plain (all-purpose) flour

2 eggs

Oil for deep-frying

Preparation time
20 minutes

Cooking time
25 minutes

Peel and finely chop the garlic. Finely chop the parsley.

Wash and steam the potatoes in their skin. (Or put in a large saucepan of salted water over high heat and bring to the boil. Reduce the heat to low and cook for 30 minutes.) Peel the cooked potatoes and mash the flesh in a medium bowl with a fork. Season with salt and pepper and add the garlic, parsley, cumin and saffron. Combine well.

Using a spoon, make medium-sized balls of mashed potato and dip them in the flour, then flatten them into patties.

Heat enough oil for deep-frying in a deep-fryer or large saucepan over high heat to 180°C (350°F), or when a cube of bread turns golden brown in 20 seconds. Deep-fry the potato cakes for 2–3 minutes, or until they are golden brown. Drain on paper towel.

Serve very hot with a salad of lettuce hearts.

POTATO PURÉE WITH OLIVE OIL

Serves 4–6

80 g (2¾ oz) butter

1 kg (2 lb 4 oz) old floury/starchy potatoes

250 ml (9 fl oz/1 cup) full-cream milk

2 sprigs thyme

1 bay leaf

160 ml (5¼ fl oz) extra virgin olive oil

Special equipment
Food mill

Preparation time
35 minutes

Cooking time
45 minutes

Cut the butter into small pieces.

Peel and wash the potatoes, and place in a large saucepan of salted water over high heat and bring to the boil. Reduce the heat to low and cook for 20–25 minutes, depending on their size.

Ten minutes before the end of the cooking time, heat the milk with the thyme and bay leaf in a small saucepan over medium heat. Strain the milk.

Drain the potatoes and put them through the food mill, adding the milk and butter pieces a little at a time.

Season with salt and pepper and mix the purée with a wooden spatula, pouring in the olive oil a little at a time. Enjoy hot served with a saucy beef dish, skewers or a pan-fried steak.

OVEN-BAKED SKIN-ON CHIPS

Serves 4

1 kg (2 lb 4 oz) medium waxy (boiling) potatoes

4 tablespoons sunflower oil

Fine sea salt

Special equipment
Vegetable brush

Tea towel (dish towel)

Preparation time
15 minutes

Cooking time
25 minutes

Preheat the oven to 180°C (350°F).

Wash the potatoes in their skin, scrubbing them with a vegetable brush to remove all the dirt. Dry the potatoes in a large tea towel (dish towel), then cut them lengthways into chips (not too thin). Dry the chips in the tea towel.

Lay the chips on a large baking tray (ideally non-stick or covered with a sheet of baking paper). Season with salt and pepper, drizzle with the oil and cook in the preheated oven for 25 minutes, turning them over occasionally.

Once the chips are brown and crispy, sprinkle them with a little fine sea salt and serve them immediately as a side for grilled meats.

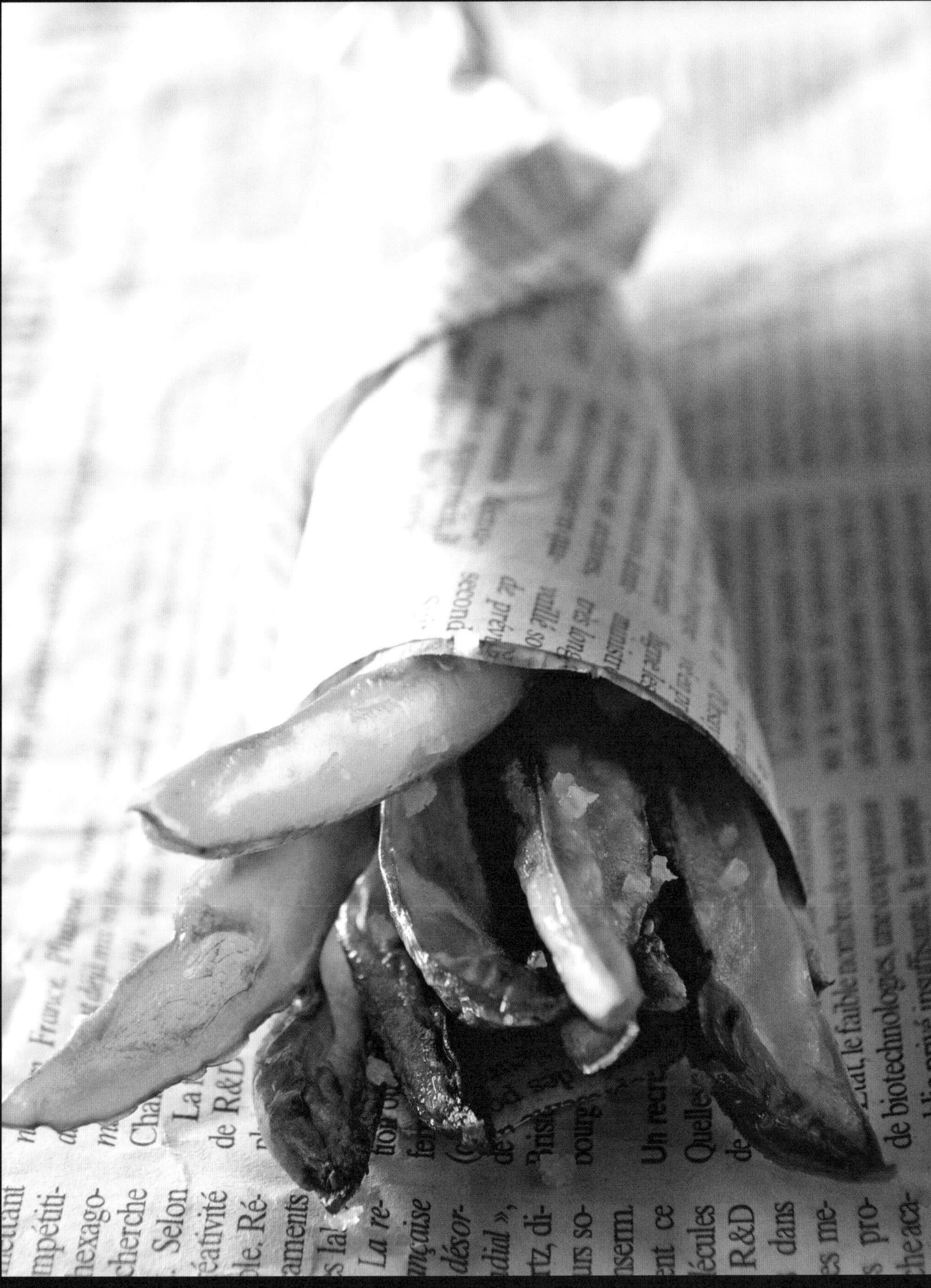

BARBECUED POTATOES WITH ROSEMARY OIL

Serves 4

5 large waxy (boiling) potatoes

2 sprigs rosemary

120 ml (3¾ fl oz) olive oil

Special equipment

Vegetable brush

Preparation time

15 minutes

Cooking time

20 minutes

Scrub the potatoes with a brush under lukewarm running water to remove all the dirt. Dry and cut them into thick slices. Lay the potato slices on a preheated hot barbecue rack. Cook them for 20 minutes, turning them from time to time so they don't burn.

Meanwhile, chop the rosemary leaves and mix them with the olive oil. Once the barbecued potatoes are cooked, place them in a large serving dish, season with salt and pepper and drizzle with the rosemary oil. Serve hot with skewers or a barbecued rib steak.

GRATED POTATO FRITTERS

Serves 4–6

1 sprig flat-leaf parsley

1 kg (2 lb 4 oz) waxy (boiling) potatoes

100 g (3½ oz) plain (all-purpose) flour

2 teaspoons baking powder

2 eggs

Oil for deep-frying

Special equipment
Food processor with grater attachment, or a cheese grater

Preparation time
35 minutes

Cooking time
10 minutes

Wash, dry and chop the parsley.

Peel and grate two of the potatoes and set aside in a medium bowl of cold water so they don't discolour.

Wash the remaining potatoes without peeling them, place in a large saucepan of salted water over high heat and bring to the boil. Reduce the heat to low and cook for 30 minutes. Drain, peel and mash the potatoes in a medium bowl. Set aside to cool.

Add the flour, baking powder, parsley and eggs to the mashed potato. Season with salt and pepper and mix well. If the mixture is too thick, add a little lukewarm water, mixing to make a smooth, homogenous batter. Add the grated potatoes and stir to combine.

Heat enough oil for deep-frying in a deep-fryer or large saucepan over high heat to 180°C (350°F), or when a cube of bread turns golden brown in 20 seconds. Drop spoonfuls of the batter and potato mixture into the oil and deep-fry. Drain the fritters on paper towel, season with salt and pepper and serve immediately on their own, with a salad or as a side for grilled meats.

MASHED POTATOES WITH HERBS

Serves 4

1 small handful chives

5 sprigs tarragon

5 sprigs flat-leaf parsley

4 large all-purpose
potatoes (about
800 g/1 lb 12 oz)

80 g (2¾ oz) salted butter

Preparation time
20 minutes

Cooking time
45 minutes

Wash, dry and chop the chives. Wash and chop the tarragon and parsley leaves. Peel the potatoes, place in a large saucepan of salted water over high heat and bring to the boil. Reduce the heat to low and cook for 25–30 minutes.

Drain the potatoes and mash with the butter in a medium bowl, using a fork. Add the herbs, mix and serve as a side for a roast.

NEW POTATOES WITH SALT AND ROSEMARY

Serves 4–6

1 kg (2 lb 4 oz) small waxy (boiling) potatoes

6 sprigs rosemary

Sunflower oil, to drizzle

Fine sea salt

Special equipment
Vegetable brush

Large ovenproof dish

Preparation time
10 minutes

Cooking time
40 minutes

Preheat the oven to 160°C (300°F).

Wash and scrub the unpeeled potatoes under cold running water. Place them in a large ovenproof dish with half the rosemary sprigs. Season with the fine sea salt and pepper, drizzle with sunflower oil and cook in the preheated oven for 40 minutes, stirring occasionally.

Chop the leaves from the remaining rosemary. Once the potatoes are well browned, tender and dry, add the chopped rosemary. Stir again and serve very hot, either with drinks or as a side for grilled meat.

CHILLI POTATOES

waxy (boiling) potatoes

100 g (3½ oz) butter

1 tablespoon curry powder

1 tablespoon chilli powder

Special equipment
Melon baller

Preparation time
40 minutes

Cooking time
25 minutes

Peel the potatoes and use a melon baller to make balls of the same size (keep the potato offcuts for a mash). Put in a large saucepan of salted water over high heat and bring to the boil. Reduce the heat to low and cook for 15 minutes. Drain.

Melt the butter in a large frying pan over medium heat until foaming. Add the potato balls, reduce the heat to low and cook for 10 minutes, without browning them too much. Insert the tip of a knife into the potatoes to check they are cooked. Season with salt and pepper and add the curry and chilli powder. Toss the potato balls to coat then remove from the heat and serve immediately with steak tartare.

SAUTÉED POTATOES WITH BACON AND ONIONS

Serves 4–6

10 sprigs flat-leaf parsley

1 kg (2 lb 4 oz) waxy
(boiling) potatoes

4 rashers rindless bacon
or 4 thick slices speck

2 large onions

2 tablespoons
sunflower oil

100 g (3½ oz) butter

Preparation time
25 minutes

Cooking time
30 minutes

Wash, dry and roughly chop the parsley leaves. Peel the potatoes and cut into cubes. Cut the bacon or speck into small chunks. Peel and slice the onions.

Heat the oil and butter in a large frying pan over medium–high heat. Add the potatoes and cook them for 15 minutes, stirring often. Once the potatoes start to brown, add the onions and bacon. Reduce the heat to low and cook for 15 minutes, stirring often. Once the potatoes are cooked and tender, add the parsley and toss through.

Serve as a main dish with a green salad or to accompany a roast or rib steak.

RÖSTI

Serves 4

500 g (1 lb 2 oz) large all-purpose potatoes

30 ml (1 fl oz) vegetable oil

50 g (1¾ oz) butter

Special equipment
Food processor with grater attachment, or a cheese grater

Preparation time
20 minutes

Cooking time
20 minutes

Peel the potatoes, wash them in cold water and grate (either by hand or in a food processor). Transfer to a medium bowl and season with salt and pepper.

Heat the oil and butter in a large frying pan or several small blini pans over medium–high heat. Add large spoonfuls of the grated potato, patting the cakes down with a spatula and pulling in the edges to make them even. Reduce the heat to medium–low and cook the rösti for 8 minutes, or until golden brown. Using a spatula, gently turn over the rösti, reduce the heat to low and cook the other side for a further 8 minutes.

Drain the rösti on paper towel and serve immediately with grilled or braised meat.

CHIPS WITH SAUCE AND CHEESE (POUTINE)

Serves 4

4 servings crispy potato chips (p. 238)

400 g (14 oz) tomme cheese (aligot, poutine or similar semi-soft cheese)

5 sprigs flat-leaf parsley (optional)

For the sauce

4 tablespoons honey

100 ml (3½ fl oz) beef broth or brown veal stock

3 tablespoons tomato sauce (ketchup)

4 tablespoons soy sauce

1 tablespoon mustard

Special equipment
Stick (hand) blender

Preparation time
20 minutes

Cooking time
35 minutes

To make the sauce, heat the honey in a small saucepan over medium–high heat. As soon as it starts to caramelise, add the broth and the tomato sauce. Bring to the boil, whisking, then add the soy sauce and mustard. Combine, reduce the heat to low and cook for 20 minutes, stirring occasionally. Season with salt and pepper and blend the sauce with a stick blender.

Divide the chips between 4 individual plates. Scatter over pieces of tomme cheese and the chopped parsley, if using, top with the sauce and serve.

POTATO SOUFFLÉ

Serves 4

480 g (1 lb 1 oz) all-purpose potatoes

250 ml (9 fl oz/1 cup) milk

150 g (5½ oz) butter

Pinch of ground nutmeg

3 egg yolks

5 egg whites

Special equipment
Food mill

Soufflé dish

Preparation time
25 minutes

Cooking time
25 minutes

Put the unpeeled potatoes in a large saucepan of salted water over high heat and bring to the boil. Reduce the heat to low and cook for 25–30 minutes. Drain and peel while the potatoes are still hot.

Warm the milk in a small saucepan over low heat. Chop half the butter into small pieces (set the remaining butter aside).

Put the potatoes through the food mill with the milk and the chopped butter. Transfer to a bowl and season with salt and pepper. Add the nutmeg then stir as the egg yolks are added. Combine well.

Preheat the oven to 180°C (350°F). Grease a large soufflé dish with the remaining butter and set aside in the refrigerator.

In a clean bowl, whisk the egg whites and a pinch of salt to soft peaks. Gently fold them into the potato purée with a large spatula.

Pour this mixture into the soufflé dish, tap it gently to settle the mixture and cook in the preheated oven for 25 minutes. Avoid opening the oven during the cooking time so the soufflé doesn't fall. Once it is well risen and golden brown, take the soufflé out of the oven and serve immediately.

POTATO AND MUSTARD SEED GRATIN

Serves 4

500 ml (17 fl oz/2 cups) thin (pouring) cream

5 tablespoons wholegrain mustard

3 tablespoons dijon mustard

800 g (1 lb 12 oz) waxy (boiling) potatoes

Butter, for greasing

Special equipment
Tea towel
(dish towel)

Preparation time
35 minutes

Cooking time
50 minutes

Put the cream and both mustards into a small saucepan over medium–high heat. Bring to the boil and remove from the heat.

Preheat the oven to 180°C (350°F). Peel the potatoes and cut into thin, even slices. Grease a large baking dish or tin with butter.

Arrange the potato slices in the dish, overlapping them around the dish to make a large rosette pattern. Season with salt and pepper and pour the mustard cream over. Cook the potatoes in the preheated oven for 45 minutes.

Prick the potatoes to check whether they are cooked – they should be slightly golden on top and soft and tender in the middle.

OLIVE OIL CHIPS WITH GARLIC AND THYME

Serves 4–6

5 pink garlic cloves (or white if not available)

1 tablespoon dried thyme

1 litre (35 fl oz/4 cups) olive oil

1 kg (2 lb 4 oz) large floury/starchy potatoes

15 sprigs lemon thyme

Preparation time
35 minutes

Cooking time
20 minutes

Bruise the garlic cloves in their skin. Wash and pick the leaves from the lemon thyme.

Heat the olive oil in a large saucepan over medium heat. Reduce the heat to low, add the garlic cloves and cook slowly for 10 minutes. Remove and drain on paper towel. When cool, peel the garlic and mix the flesh with the dried thyme.

Peel and wash the potatoes. Cut them into long, thin, evenly sized chips. Wash them in cold water and dry them well in a large tea towel (dish towel). Increase the heat to high and bring the oil to 150°C (300°F), or when a cube of bread turns golden-brown in 40 seconds. Deep-fry the chips in the hot oil in two or three batches. Set aside on paper towel to cool completely.

At serving time, reheat the oil to 190°C (375°F), or when a cube of bread turns golden-brown in 10 seconds. Deep-fry the chips again, stirring from time to time, for 4–5 minutes, or until crispy and golden brown. Drain on paper towel.

Transfer the hot chips to a large bowl, add the dried thyme and garlic mixture and the lemon thyme leaves. Season with salt and toss gently to combine. Serve the chips immediately, on their own with drinks or as a side to grilled meat.

DAUPHINE POTATOES

Serves 4–6

4 medium
floury/starchy potatoes

400 ml (14 fl oz) milk

70 g (2½ oz) butter

300 g (10½ oz) plain
(all-purpose) flour

3 eggs

Oil for deep-frying

Preparation time
45 minutes

Resting time
15 minutes

Cooking time
20 minutes

Peel the potatoes, put in a large saucepan of salted water over high heat and bring to the boil. Reduce the heat to low and cook for 25–30 minutes. Drain and mash the potatoes until smooth. Transfer to a medium bowl and set aside at room temperature.

Put the milk, butter, 2 pinches salt and 1 pinch pepper into a medium saucepan over medium–high heat and bring to the boil. Add the flour and mix vigorously until the dough comes away from the sides of the saucepan and is lump-free. Remove from the heat and add the eggs one at a time, mixing with a wooden spatula to thoroughly incorporate between additions. Add the mashed potato and mix again to combine well. Set the mixture aside to rest at room temperature for 15 minutes.

Put enough oil for deep-frying in a large saucepan over high heat. Heat to 170°C (325°F), or when a cube of bread turns golden brown in 20 seconds. Make small balls of dough using a spoon and drop into the oil, five at a time. Deep-fry, turning the balls so they cook evenly, for 2–3 minutes, or until golden brown. Drain the dauphine potatoes on paper towel and serve immediately with grilled meat.

CHEESE-TOPPED POTATO TIAN

Serves 4

4 large waxy (boiling) potatoes

3 onions

8 pink garlic cloves (or white if not available)

3 tomatoes (not too ripe)

2 zucchini (courgettes)

1 eggplant (aubergine)

120 ml (4 fl oz/½ cup) olive oil

3 bay leaves

1 tablespoon dried thyme leaves

200 g (7 oz) grated cheddar cheese

Special equipment
Mandoline
(or large sharp knife)

Large baking dish or tin

Preparation time
30 minutes

Cooking time
45 minutes

Peel the potatoes and slice thinly using a mandoline or large sharp knife. Set aside in a bowl of cold water to prevent discolouration. Peel and slice the onions and garlic. Slice the tomatoes, zucchini and eggplant into thin rounds.

Pour 2 tablespoons of the olive oil into the bottom of a baking dish or tin. Arrange the potatoes, onion, tomatoes, zucchinis and eggplant in the dish in vertical layers, packing the rows tightly, as the vegetables will shrink during cooking.

Preheat the oven to 170°C (325°F).

Insert the garlic and bay leaves between the rows of vegetables, sprinkle with the thyme, season with salt and pepper and drizzle the remaining olive oil over.

Scatter the grated cheese over and cook in the preheated oven for 45 minutes, or until the cheese has browned slightly and the vegetables are soft and tender. Cool to warm and serve as a side for a baked fish.

BOULANGÈRE POTATOES

Serves 4–6

1 kg (2 lb 4 oz)
floury/starchy potatoes

4 onions

100 g (3½ oz) butter

4 sprigs thyme

2 bay leaves

500 ml (17 fl oz/2 cups)
beef stock

Preparation time
35 minutes

Cooking time
45 minutes

Peel the potatoes and slice them into thin rounds. Peel and slice the onions. Preheat the oven to 180°C (350°F).

Butter the base of a baking dish or tin (reserve some butter to dot over the top) and cover with a thick layer of potato slices. Season with salt and pepper, cover with the onion slices, 2 sprigs of the thyme and 1 of the bay leaves. Make another layer of potatoes, season with salt and pepper and add the remaining thyme and bay leaf.

Pour the stock over, place a few pieces of butter on top, then cook in the preheated oven for 45 minutes, until the potatoes are tender (check with the tip of a knife). Adjust the seasoning and serve as a main meal with a salad or as a side for a rib or other steak.

POTATOES IN A CLAY POT

Serves 4

1 kg (2 lb 4 oz) small, waxy (boiling) potatoes

5 sprigs thyme

200 g sel gris (coarse grey sea salt) or other coarse sea salt

Special equipment
Vegetable brush

Tea towel (dish towel)

Diable (clay pot) or casserole dish

Preparation time
10 minutes

Cooking time
50 minutes

Preheat the oven to 170°C (325°F).

Wash the potatoes under cold running water, scrubbing them with a vegetable brush. Dry in a large tea towel (dish towel). Place the potatoes in a clay pot or casserole dish. Moisten the thyme with a little cold water, combine with the salt and scatter over the potatoes.

Cook in the preheated oven for 50 minutes, or until the potatoes are dry and crispy. Serve as a side for a rib steak or skewers.

GARLIC POTATOES

(boiling) potatoes

100 g (3½ oz) goose

Preparation time
20 minutes

Cooking time
40 minutes

Wash and roughly chop the parsley leaves. Peel and crush the garlic cloves. Peel the potatoes and slice them into thin rounds.

Heat the goose fat in a large frying pan over medium heat. Add the potatoes and cook, stirring occasionally, for 20 minutes.

Add the parsley and garlic, season with salt and pepper, and toss gently to combine. Reduce the heat to low and cook, stirring occasionally, for a further 20 minutes, until golden and tender.

Serve immediately with a rib eye steak.

WAFFLE-CUT POTATOES

Serves 4–6

1 kg (2 lb 4 oz) large (all-purpose) potatoes

Oil for deep-frying

Special equipment
Mandoline
(or large sharp knife)

Tea towel
(dish towel)

Preparation time
15 minutes

Cooking time
20 minutes

Peel and wash the potatoes, then cut them into evenly sized waffled slices ('gaufrettes') using a mandoline (rotate 90° with each cut). Wash in cold water and dry well in a large tea towel (dish towel).

Put enough oil for deep-frying in a deep-fryer or large saucepan. Heat to 180°C (350°F) over high heat, or when a cube of bread turns golden brown in 15 seconds. Deep-fry the potato slices for 4–5 minutes, stirring constantly, until crispy and golden brown. Drain on paper towel and season with salt. Serve with drinks, or as a side for a steak or roast.

THIN-SHAVED POTATO CRISPS

Serves 4–6

1 kg (2 lb 4 oz) large waxy (boiling) potatoes

Oil for deep-frying

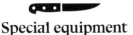

Special equipment

Deep-fryer or large saucepan

Spider strainer

Preparation time

40 minutes

2–3 minutes

Peel, wash and dry the potatoes. Using a sharp vegetable peeler, peel the potatoes, gently turning to make large shavings (a bit like peeling an apple in one continuous strip).

Put enough oil for deep-frying in a deep-fryer or large saucepan. Heat to 180°C (350°F) over high heat, or when a cube of bread turns golden brown in 15 seconds. Deep-fry the potato shavings in several batches, stirring with a spider strainer to prevent clumping, for 2–3 minutes or until golden brown. Drain on paper towel, season with salt and pepper and serve immediately.

BEEF & POTATOES

BEEF AND POTATOES

At this point, the equation becomes even more complex. You've realised by now that there is nothing simple about beef. Potatoes, ditto. So, clearly, the beef-and-potato combination is not going to be handed to you on a plate. You don't serve chips with boiled meat, as a rule. Neither do you serve potato crisps alongside a saucy meat dish, as a matter of principle. But you can escape the prospect of enjoying nothing but steak and chips alone for eternity without abandoning the sanctity of the beef-and-potato union. Think about it: classic cottage pie – not much more than beef and potatoes. And then there's *bún bò* (sliced beef, salad, herbs and chips), pot-au-feu with purple potatoes, a tagine of beef and potato served with mint yoghurt…just some of the beef-and-potato dishes that will serve to broaden your culinary horizons, and transform you from a gastronomically limited steak-and-chips kind of person to a cosmopolitan daredevil foodie – all without forsaking your two favourite food groups. You will, in short, develop your adventurous side while both feet stay firmly planted in the beef-and-potato camp. Embrace it. Get stuck in.

CLASSIC COTTAGE PIE

Serves 5–7

1 kg (2 lb 4 oz) floury/starchy or mashing potatoes

200 ml (7 fl oz) hot milk

80 g (2¾ oz) butter

2 large onions

2 garlic cloves

4 tablespoons olive oil

1 teaspoon dried herbs de Provence or mixed dried herbs

300 g (10½ oz) sausage meat

70 g (2½ oz) tomato paste (concentrated purée)

800 g (1 lb 12 oz) minced (ground) beef

3 tablespoons breadcrumbs (optional)

Special equipment
Food mill

Preparation time
20 minutes

Cooking time
1 hour 10 minutes

Peel the potatoes, place in a large saucepan of salted water over high heat and bring to the boil. Reduce the heat to low and cook for 15–20 minutes. Drain, reserving the cooking water, and put the potatoes through a food mill. Transfer to a medium bowl and add a little of the cooking water, the hot milk and butter. Season with salt and pepper, stir to combine and set aside.

Peel and chop the onions and garlic. Heat the oil in a large frying pan over medium–high heat. Add the onion, garlic, dried herbs and sausage meat, reduce the heat to low and cook for 10 minutes, stirring occasionally. Add the tomato paste and minced beef. Mix together and cook for a further 8–10 minutes.

Preheat the oven to 180°C (350°F). Spoon the meat mixture into a large baking dish. Cover with the potato purée. Sprinkle with breadcrumbs, if using, and cook in the preheated oven for 30 minutes.

Serve the cottage pie hot with a green salad dressed with a strong mustard vinaigrette.

BEEF WELLINGTON

Serves 4 ◆ 1.5 kg (3 lb 5 oz) beef tenderloin \ 2 tablespoons grapeseed oil \ 1 garlic clove \ 2 French shallots \ 700 g (1 lb 9 oz) mushrooms \ 80 g (2¾ oz) butter \ 200 g (7 oz) minced (ground) veal \ 1 sheet (25 x 50 cm/ 10 x 20 inches) frozen puff pastry, thawed \ 1 beaten egg yolk

■▬ Preparation time ◆ 35 minutes

❀ Cooking time ◆ 35 minutes

⏱ Resting time for meat ◆ 5 minutes

Season the beef with salt and pepper. Heat the oil in a large frying pan over medium–high heat. Add the meat and cook, turning, until browned on all sides. Transfer to a plate and allow to cool completely. Wipe out the frying pan. Peel and chop the garlic and shallots. Wash and chop the mushrooms.

Melt the butter in the pan over medium–high heat. Add the garlic, shallots and mushrooms and cook, stirring, until any liquid has completely evaporated (the mixture must be quite dry). Season with salt and pepper and set aside to cool completely. Add the minced veal and mix well.

Preheat the oven to 170°C (325°F). Lay the sheet of puff pastry on a work surface and spread with the mushroom mixture. Place the beef fillet on top and roll up tightly. Place the wellington in a baking dish. Mix the egg yolk with 1 tablespoon water and brush over the pastry. Cook in the preheated oven for 25 minutes.

Once the beef wellington is cooked and golden, remove the baking dish from the oven, cover with foil and let it rest for 5 minutes. Cut into thick slices and serve with duchess potatoes.

DUCHESS POTATOES

Serves 4–6 ◆ 1 kg (2 lb 4 oz) large all-purpose potatoes \ 100 g (3½ oz) salted butter \ 1 pinch nutmeg / 3 egg yolks \ Vegetable oil for greasing

◀▬▬ Special equipment ◆ Food mill \ Piping bag

■▬ Preparation time ◆ 30 minutes

❀ Cooking time ◆ 50 minutes

Peel and wash the potatoes and cut them in half. Put in a large saucepan of salted water over high heat and bring to the boil. Reduce the heat to low and cook for 40 minutes. Drain the potatoes and put them through the food mill, adding the butter in small pieces. Transfer to a medium bowl, add the nutmeg and season with salt and pepper. Mix with a wooden spatula to a smooth purée and set aside to cool a little.

Preheat the oven to 200°C (400°F). Lightly grease a baking tray with vegetable oil.

Add the egg yolks to the potato purée one at a time, using the spatula to mix through after each addition. Fill a piping bag with the purée and pipe out small rosettes on the oiled tray. Cook in the preheated oven for 3–4 minutes, or until warmed through and golden brown on top.

MEXICAN-STYLE BRAISED BEEF

Serves 4–6

1.2 kg (2 lb 11 oz)
stewing beef (blade,
chuck or shin)

1 small handful
coriander (cilantro)

2 onions

4 garlic cloves

2 red capsicums (peppers)

1 small green chilli

200 g (7 oz) flat beans

600 g (1 lb 5 oz) medium
all-purpose potatoes

2 large tomatoes

1 tablespoon
ground cumin

2 tablespoons corn oil,
or sunflower or canola oil

1 tablespoon plain
(all-purpose) flour

500 ml (17 fl oz/2 cups)
beef broth

Cut the meat into large cubes. Wash and chop the coriander leaves. Peel and chop the onions and garlic. De-stem and slice the capsicums and chilli. Cut the flat beans in half. Peel the potatoes, cut the larger ones in half and set aside in a bowl of cold water. Chop the tomatoes.

Combine the meat cubes with the garlic, onion, cumin, 1 tablespoon of the oil and the coriander in a bowl. Cover and marinate for 2 hours in the refrigerator.

Heat the remaining oil in a casserole dish over high heat. Add the meat and marinade and cook, stirring, for 2–3 minutes. Add the flour, capsicum, chilli and tomatoes and cook, stirring continuously, for 5 minutes. Add the broth, stir through and reduce the heat to low. Simmer, covered, for 1 hour 30 minutes, or until the meat is cooked and tender.

Transfer the pieces of meat to a bowl and add 200 ml (7 fl oz) water to the cooking liquid. Blend the sauce using a stick blender. Season with salt and pepper, return the meat to the casserole dish and add the potatoes and flat beans. Simmer for 30 minutes over low heat, adding a little water if the sauce is too thick. Adjust the seasoning and serve immediately.

Preparation time
35 minutes

Resting time
2 hours

Cooking time
2 hours 10 minutes

BEEF AND POTATO BURGERS WITH SPICY SAUCE

Makes 4 hamburgers

4 tablespoons tomato sauce (ketchup)

5 drops Tabasco sauce

1 large oxheart tomato

1 kg (2 lb 4 oz) waxy (boiling) potatoes

2 eggs

1 tablespoon plain (all-purpose) flour

3 tablespoons olive oil

4 meat burgers (p. 24)

4 slices mimolette or hard aged cheddar cheese

8 large basil leaves

Special equipment
Food processor

Preparation time
30 minutes

Cooking time
30–35 minutes

Combine the tomato sauce and Tabasco sauce. Cut the tomato into thick slices.

Peel the potatoes and grate in a food processor. Whisk the eggs and flour together in a mixing bowl and season with salt and pepper. Add the grated potatoes and combine. Make 8 potato patties the size of a hamburger bun.

Heat the oil in a large frying pan over medium–high heat. Add the potato patties and cook for 2–3 minutes on each side. Reduce the heat to low and cook for 25 minutes.

Transfer the potato cakes to a plate lined with paper towel. Add the meat burgers to the frying pan, increase the heat to medium–high and cook to your taste.

To assemble the burgers, use a potato pancake for the base and spread with a spoonful of sauce. Top with a meat burger, a slice of cheese, a slice of tomato, 2 basil leaves and another potato cake. Serve immediately.

ROASTED KIPFLER POTATOES WITH DRIED BEEF

Serves 4–6

800 g (1 lb 12 oz) kipfler (fingerling) potatoes

10 thin slices pastrami (or air-dried beef such as bresaola), about 100 g (3½ oz)

salted butter

2 tablespoons sunflower oil

Special equipment
Vegetable brush

Tea towel (dish towel)

Preparation time
35 minutes

Cooking time
45 minutes

Preheat the oven to 170°C (325°F). Scrub the potatoes with a brush under cold running water to clean well, and dry in a large tea towel (dish towel).

Place the potatoes in a single layer in a large baking dish. Season with salt and pepper and cook in the preheated oven for 30 minutes, turning the potatoes regularly. Meanwhile, cut the slices of dried beef into wide strips.

When cooked, set aside the potatoes to cool.

Wrap each potato twice around with a strip of dried beef so it holds well. Ten minutes before serving time, melt the butter in a large frying pan over medium heat until foaming. Reduce the heat to low, add the wrapped potatoes and cook for 6–8 minutes, turning them gently and basting them with the butter. Serve hot with drinks, or with a green salad.

PAPRIKA BEEF AND POTATO CROQUETTES

Serves 4

600 g (1 lb 5 oz) large all-purpose potatoes

4 sprigs flat-leaf parsley

4 garlic cloves

3 eggs

½ teaspoon chilli powder

2 tablespoons plain (all-purpose) flour

1 tablespoon paprika, plus extra for dusting

500 g (1 lb 2 oz) minced (ground) beef

Breadcrumbs for coating

Oil for deep-frying

Special equipment
Deep-fryer (or large saucepan)

Preparation time
45 minutes

Resting time
30 minutes

Cooking time
45 minutes

Peel the potatoes, place in a large saucepan of salted water over high heat and bring to the boil. Reduce the heat to low and cook for 25–30 minutes.

Wash and chop the parsley leaves. Crush the garlic. Whisk the eggs.

Drain the potatoes, transfer to a large bowl and mash. Add the chilli powder, flour, paprika, parsley, garlic, eggs and minced meat. Mix together well, shape into small balls and place on a large plate. Set aside, uncovered, in the refrigerator for 30 minutes.

Put enough oil for deep-frying in a large deep-fryer or saucepan over high heat. Heat to 170°C (325°F), or when a cube of bread turns golden brown in 20 seconds.

Roll the meatballs in the breadcrumbs and deep-fry them, five at a time, for 3–4 minutes, or until golden and crunchy. Drain the croquettes on paper towel, season with salt and pepper and dust with paprika. Serve immediately with a green salad.

CHEESY BEEF AND POTATO BAKE

Serves 4–6

2 garlic cloves

3 tablespoons crème fraîche

Pinch of nutmeg

400 g (14 oz) rump steak

180 g (6 oz) washed rind cheese (such as Taleggio, Epoisses or Pont-l'Evêque)

600 g (1 lb 5 oz) small waxy (boiling) potatoes

50 g (1¾ oz) butter

Special equipment

Garlic crusher

Vegetable brush

Preparation time

25 minutes

Cooking time

40 minutes

Peel and crush the garlic. Whisk the crème fraîche in a bowl with a little salt, the nutmeg and the garlic. Cut the meat into small slices. Cut the cheese into thick slices.

Scrub the potatoes with a vegetable brush to remove all the dirt. Put them in a large saucepan of salted water over high heat and bring to the boil. Reduce the heat to low and cook for 25–30 minutes. Drain and cut the potatoes in half lengthways.

Preheat the oven to 180°C (350°F). Put the potatoes in a baking dish, dot with the butter, season with salt and pepper and cook in the preheated oven for 10 minutes. Once the potatoes start to brown, take the dish out of the oven, add the garlic cream mixture and scatter the pieces of beef and cheese on top. Brown under the oven grill (broiler) for 5–8 minutes, until the meat is lightly cooked and the cheese is melted. Serve very hot, with a green salad.

POT-AU-FEU WITH PURPLE POTATOES

Serves 6–8

2 kg (4 lb 8 oz) stewing beef (shin, blade, chuck or chuck tenderloin)

1 bouquet garni

1 handful coarse salt

2 sweet potatoes

8 small purple potatoes

For the sauce

1 small handful flat-leaf parsley, plus extra to garnish

4 sprigs tarragon

5 cornichons (small gherkins/pickles)

1 small handful chives

3 small French shallots

2 hard-boiled eggs

1 tablespoon small capers

100 ml (3½ fl oz) olive oil

2 tablespoons white wine vinegar

Fine sea salt

Preparation time
40 minutes

Cooking time
3 hours 30 minutes

Heat 5 litres (175 fl oz/20 cups) water in a large saucepan over high heat. Cut the meat into chunks, add to the saucepan and bring to the boil for 3–4 minutes. Drain the meat, discarding the cooking water, and rinse with clean water. Return the meat to the clean pot over medium–high heat and add water to 5 cm (2 inches) above the level of the meat. Add the bouquet garni and coarse salt, bring to the boil then reduce the heat to low and simmer for 2 hours.

Peel the sweet potatoes and purple potatoes. Put them in a large saucepan of salted water over high heat and bring to the boil. Reduce the heat to low and cook for 25 minutes. Drain and set aside.

To make the sauce, wash and roughly chop the parsley and tarragon leaves. Chop the cornichons. Wash and chop the chives. Slice the shallots. Mash the eggs. Combine the capers, cornichons, all of the herbs, shallots and mashed egg in a mixing bowl. Add the olive oil and vinegar, season with salt and pepper, and mix together. Cover and set the mixture aside to marinate at room temperature.

At the end of the pot-au-feu cooking time, add the sweet and purple potatoes to the broth for 5 minutes to reheat them. Arrange the pieces of meat and potatoes on a large dish with the broth on the side. Chop the extra parsley and scatter over as a garnish. Serve very hot with pieces of toast and the sauce on the side.

BEEF AND POTATO CROQUETTES

Serves 4

500 g (1 lb 2 oz) boneless beef (inside round/topside)

4 garlic cloves

20 g (¾ oz) ginger

½ teaspoon tamarind powder

1 large onion

5 green chillies

500 ml (17 fl oz/2 cups) coconut oil

500 g (1 lb 2 oz) all-purpose potatoes

2 eggs

5 tablespoons breadcrumbs

Special equipment
Pressure cooker

Food processor

Preparation time
30 minutes

Cooking time
50 minutes

Cook the cubed meat, peeled garlic cloves, half the peeled ginger and the tamarind powder in a pressure cooker for 15–20 minutes. Cool slightly and process the cooked mixture in a food processor and set aside.

Chop the onion. Seed the chillies. Slice the remaining ginger.

Heat 2 tablespoons of the coconut oil in a frying pan over medium–high heat. Add the onion, chillies and remaining ginger and cook until dark brown. Add the processed meat mixture, season with salt and pepper and cook for 3–4 minutes. Set aside.

Peel the potatoes. Put them in a large saucepan of salted water over high heat and bring to the boil. Reduce the heat to low and cook for 25 minutes.

Drain the potatoes and crush with a fork. Combine with the meat mixture and shape into flat croquettes.

Beat the eggs in a bowl. Dip the croquettes in the egg mixture, then in the breadcrumbs.

Put the remaining coconut oil in a large saucepan over high heat. Heat to 170°C (325°F), or when a cube of bread turns golden brown in 20 seconds. Deep fry the croquettes for 2–3 minutes, or until golden brown. Serve immediately.

POTATO PIE WITH DRIED BEEF

Serves 4–6

5 sprigs flat-leaf parsley

4 garlic cloves

500 g (1 lb 2 oz) floury/starchy potatoes

300 ml (10½ fl oz) crème fraîche

Pinch of nutmeg

1 egg

2 sheets (25 x 50 cm/ 10 x 20 inches) frozen puff pastry, thawed

10 thin slices pastrami (or air-dried beef such as bresaola)

Preparation time
35 minutes

Cooking time
1 hour 15 minutes

Wash and chop the parsley leaves. Peel and chop the garlic. Peel the potatoes and slice them thinly.

Put the potato slices, crème fraîche, garlic, parsley and nutmeg in a medium bowl. Combine gently.

Preheat the oven to 200°C (400°F). Line a baking tray with baking paper. Whisk the egg with a little cold water and set aside.

Place a sheet of puff pastry on the baking tray. Lay the slices of dried beef over the pastry and cover with the potato slices. Top with the second sheet of puff pastry. Brush the edges with a little of the egg mixture and press together with your fingertips to seal. Brush the top of the pie with the remaining egg mixture.

Reduce the oven temperature to 180°C (350°F) and bake the pie for 1 hour 15 minutes, or until cooked through and golden brown.

Let the pie cool for a few minutes before serving.

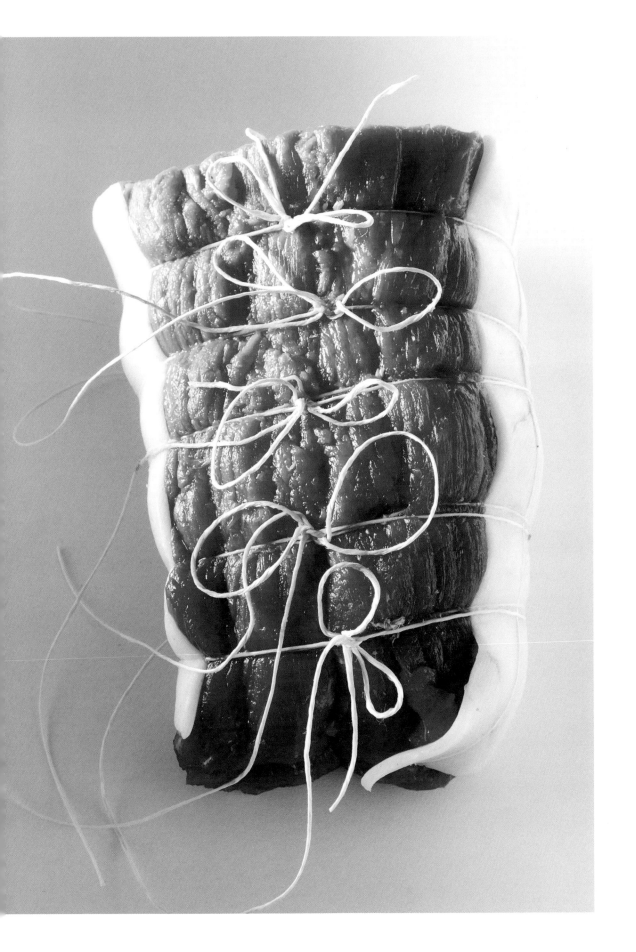

BRAISED OXTAIL AND POTATO PIE

Serves 4–6

2 large onions

4 garlic cloves

4 large tomatoes

80 g (2¾ oz) butter

4 tablespoons sunflower oil

2.5 kg (5 lb 8 oz) oxtail, cut into thick slices

1 sprig thyme

2 bay leaves

500 ml (17 fl oz/2 cups) red wine

3 tablespoons breadcrumbs

For the potato purée

1 kg (2 lb 4 oz) large floury/starchy potatoes

80 g (2¾ oz) butter

2 tablespoons crème fraîche

Special equipment
Cast-iron casserole dish

Preparation time
35 minutes

Cooking time
2 hours 45 minutes

Peel and slice the onions. Bruise the garlic cloves in their skin. Chop the tomatoes.

Heat the butter and oil in a large cast-iron casserole dish over medium–high heat. Add the oxtail, onion, garlic, thyme and bay leaves and cook, stirring, for 3–4 minutes. Season with salt and pepper, add the wine and cook until the liquid is reduce by a quarter. Add the tomatoes, stir through, reduce the heat to low and braise gently for 2 hours, until the meat is cooked.

Remove the meat from the cooking liquid and set aside to cool. Increase the heat to medium–high and reduce the remaining cooking liquid by a quarter. Set aside.

Discard the bones and shred the cooled meat.

Meanwhile, to make the potato purée, peel the potatoes and put them in a large saucepan of salted water over high heat and bring to the boil. Reduce the heat to low and cook for 25 minutes.

Preheat the oven to 180°C (350°F).

Drain the potatoes, transfer to a medium bowl and mash with the butter and crème fraîche. Season with salt and pepper.

Place the meat in a large baking dish. Add the reduced cooking liquid and mix through. Cover with the potato purée and sprinkle with breadcrumbs. Bake the pie in the preheated oven for 45 minutes. Serve the pie directly from the baking dish.

Suggestion
Serve with a green salad.

RISSOLE SANDWICHES

Makes 4

400 g (14 oz) crispy potato chips (p. 238)

600 g (1 lb 5 oz) minced (ground) beef

A few green lettuce leaves

120 g (4¼ oz) tomato sauce (ketchup)

1 teaspoon Tabasco sauce

1 tablespoon herbs de Provence or mixed dried herbs

4 individual baguettes

Special equipment
4 skewers

Preparation time
20 minutes

Cooking time
20 minutes

Make the chips and set aside in a warm place.

If using wooden skewers, soak them in water until ready to use.

Season the meat with salt and pepper and knead until smooth. Wrap the meat around the skewers and set aside in the refrigerator. Wash, dry and shred the lettuce. Combine the tomato sauce, Tabasco sauce and dried herbs in a small bowl.

Preheat the oven grill (broiler) or the barbecue to medium–high heat. Place the meat skewers on a baking tray and cook for 5 minutes, turning to cook evenly.

Split the baguettes and warm them in the oven. Brush them inside with the sauce, then fill with shredded lettuce leaves and crispy chips. Add a meat skewer to each sandwich with a little more sauce. Squeeze the bread together to remove the skewer from the meat and serve with napkins on the side.

Suggestion
To save time, you can use precooked frozen chips.

BEEF AND POTATO PUFF PASTRY ROLL

Serves 4

1 handful tarragon

500 g (1 lb 2 oz) large floury/starchy potatoes

1 sheet (25 x 50 cm/ 10 x 20 inches) frozen puff pastry, thawed

2 tablespoons strong mustard

700 g (1 lb 9 oz) minced (ground) beef

Olive oil for drizzling

Special equipment
Mandoline
(or large sharp knife)

Preparation time
25 minutes

Cooking time
45 minutes

Wash and chop the tarragon leaves. Peel the potatoes and cut them into very thin slices using a mandoline or large sharp knife. Preheat the oven to 180°C (350°F).

Lay the puff pastry on a work surface, brush with mustard and scatter over some tarragon. Cover with a layer of potatoes, then a layer of minced meat. Drizzle over a little olive oil, than add another layer of potato slices, and another layer of meat, repeating until the ingredients run out.

Fold in the edges of the pastry, then roll up to make a large, even roll. Place on a large baking tray. Reduce the oven temperature to 170°C (325°F) and bake the pastry roll for 45 minutes, or until the potato is cooked in the centre when pricked with a skewer.

To serve, cut the roll into thick slices with a serrated knife.

Suggestion
Serve with a green salad or green beans.

BEEF AND POTATO LASAGNE

Serves 6–8

3 garlic cloves

1 kg (2 lb 4 oz) large
waxy (boiling) potatoes

250 g (9 oz)
mozzarella balls

1 large handful basil

900 g (2 lb) minced
(ground) beef

1 teaspoon dried thyme

100 ml (3½ fl oz) passata
(puréed tomatoes)

3 tablespoons olive oil

100 g (3½ oz) grated
parmesan cheese

Special equipment
Mandoline
(or large sharp knife)

Preparation time
35 minutes

Cooking time
1 hour

Peel and crush the garlic. Peel the potatoes and cut into very thin slices using a mandoline or a large sharp knife. Thinly slice the mozzarella. Wash and roughly chop the basil leaves.

Combine the minced beef with the garlic, basil, thyme and passata in a mixing bowl. Season with salt and pepper.

Preheat the oven to 170°C (325°F).

Pour the olive oil into a baking dish. Place a layer of potato in the bottom of the dish, spread a layer of meat about 2.5 cm (1 inch) thick, on top, then scatter around a few slices of mozzarella. Cover with another potato layer, another meat layer and more mozzarella. Repeat this process until you run out of ingredients, finishing with a layer of potato. Sprinkle with the parmesan and bake in the preheated oven for 1 hour, or when the potato is tender when pricked in the centre with a skewer.

Allow the lasagne to cool a little before serving.

Suggestion
Serve with a green salad.

ALSATIAN BEEF AND POTATO CASSEROLE

Serves 6–8

1.5 kg (3 lb 5 oz) beef top blade

3 large onions

5 garlic cloves

750 ml (26 fl oz/3 cups) red wine

6 sprigs thyme

4 bay leaves

1 kg (2 lb 4 oz) waxy (boiling) potatoes

2 tablespoons plain (all-purpse) flour

Special equipment
Large earthenware baking dish with lid

Preparation time
40 minutes

Resting time
24 hours

Cooking time
3 hours

The day before, cut the meat into large cubes. Peel and slice the onions and garlic. Put the meat, onions, garlic, red wine, thyme and bay leaves in a large bowl. Stir to combine, cover and marinate in the refrigerator overnight.

The next day, preheat the oven to 180°C (350°F). Peel the potatoes and slice into thin rounds.

Transfer the meat and marinade to a large earthenware baking dish with a lid. Add the potato slices, mix through and season with salt and pepper. Cover the dish with its lid and apply a light dough made with the flour and a little water to create a seal.

Reduce the oven temperature to 170°C (325°F). Cook the casserole for 3 hours.

Place the casserole dish on the table, break open the seal, remove the lid and serve immediately.

BEEF AND POTATO FONDUE

Serves 4

1 kg (2 lb 4 oz) large floury/starchy potatoes

50 ml (1¾ fl oz) white wine

2 sprigs thyme

1 bay leaf

200 g (7 oz) strong gruyère cheese

2 tablespoons crème fraîche

1 pinch nutmeg

800 g (1 lb 12 oz) flank, hanger or skirt steak

2 tablespoons vegetable oil

Special equipment
Stick (hand) blender

Fondue forks or skewers

Preparation time
35 minutes

Cooking time
45 minutes

Peel the potatoes and cut into chunks. Put them in a large saucepan with 100 ml (3½ fl oz) water, the white wine, thyme and bay leaf. Bring to the boil over medium–high heat, then reduce heat to low and cook until the potato is tender. Remove and discard the thyme and bay leaf. Purée the potato mixture with a stick blender until smooth.

Remove the rind from the cheese and grate. Add to the warm potato purée with the crème fraîche and mix with a spatula until the cheese has melted. Season with salt and pepper, add the nutmeg and stir through. Set aside in a warm place.

Cut the meat into small pieces and season with salt and pepper. Heat the oil in a large frying pan over high heat. Add the pieces of meat and cook for 2–3 minutes. Transfer to a large plate and enjoy in the same way as a fondue, dipping the pieces of meat on the end of fondue forks or skewers into the cheesy potato purée.

POTATOES BOLOGNESE

Serves 4

2 large onions

5 garlic cloves

1 kg (2 lb 4 oz) small
waxy (boiling) potatoes

4 tablespoons olive oil

500 ml (17 fl oz/2 cups)
passata (puréed tomatoes)

4 sprigs thyme

2 bay leaves

700 g (1 lb 9 oz) minced
(ground) beef

Special equipment
Flame-proof
casserole dish

Preparation time
35 minutes

Cooking time
45 minutes

Peel and chop the onions and garlic. Peel the potatoes.

Heat the oil in a casserole dish over high heat. Add the onion and garlic and cook for 2–3 minutes. Add the passata and stir to combine. Add the potatoes, thyme, bay leaves and 400 ml (14 fl oz) water. Stir to combine, reduce the heat to low and cook for 25 minutes.

Add the minced beef to the casserole dish, stir to combine and cook for a further 20 minutes, stirring occasionally, over low heat. Adjust the seasoning and serve immediately.

ROAST BEEF AND POTATO CRISP BAGUETTE WITH ONION RINGS

Makes 4 serves

¼ cucumber

4 slices roast beef

4 sprigs watercress

2 large onions

100 ml (3½ fl oz) milk

40 g (1½ oz) plain (all-purpose) flour

Oil for deep-frying

½ baguette

2 teaspoons strong mustard

150 g (5½ oz) freshly made cooked potato crisps (p. 242)

Preparation time
10 minutes

Cooking time
10 minutes

Preheat the oven to 180°C (350°F).

Wash, seed and slice the cucumber. Slice the roast beef into thin strips. Wash and dry the watercress. Peel and slice the onion.

Dip the onion slices in the milk and then the flour. Place on a plate.

Put enough oil for deep-frying in a deep-fryer or large saucepan over high heat. Heat to 170°C (325°F), or when a cube of bread turns golden brown in 20 seconds. Cook the onion rings for 2–3 minutes, or until crisp and golden, and drain on paper towel.

Cut the baguette into four pieces and heat in the preheated oven for 2–3 minutes. Split the baguette pieces and spread with mustard. Place the strips of roast beef inside, add 2–3 onion rings, and some cucumber slices, watercress and potato crisps. Season with salt and pepper and serve warm.

MARINATED STEAK TARTARE WITH FRIED POTATOES

Serves 4

4 spring onions (scallions)

800 g (1 lb 12 oz) minced (ground) beef

4 tablespoons soy sauce

100 ml (3½ fl oz) olive oil

1 organic lime

600 g (1 lb 5 oz) small new potatoes

Oil for deep-frying

Special equipment
Zester

Tea towel
(dish towel)

Resting time
15 minutes

Preparation time
15 minutes

Cooking time
25 minutes

Trim and finely shred the spring onions, including the stems.

Put the minced beef, soy sauce, olive oil and spring onion in a large bowl. Add the grated zest of the lime, then squeeze the lime and add the juice. Season with salt and pepper and mix the ingredients together well. Cover and set aside in the refrigerator for 15 minutes.

Meanwhile, scrub the potatoes under a cold running water to remove the dirt. Dry with a large tea towel (dish towel) and cut in half.

Put enough oil for deep-frying in a deep-fryer or large saucepan over high heat. Heat to 170°C (325°F), or when a cube of bread turns golden brown in 20 seconds. Cook the potato halves for 2–3 minutes, or until crisp and golden. Drain on paper towel and sprinkle with salt.

Serve the chilled meat with the golden crunchy potatoes.

BEEF AND POTATO TAGINE

Serves 4

4 large red onions

5 pink garlic cloves (or white if not available)

800 g (1 lb 12 oz) all-purpose potatoes

800 g (1 lb 12 oz) minced (ground) beef

2 tablespoons ground cumin

1 tablespoon curry powder

120 ml (3¾ fl oz) olive oil

2 tablespoons honey

2 sprigs thyme

For the sauce

5 sprigs mint

4 tablespoons olive oil

150 g (5½ oz) plain yoghurt

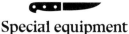

Special equipment
Tagine (or a large cast-iron dish with lid)

Preparation time
35 minutes

Cooking time
50 minutes

To make the sauce, wash and chop the mint. Combine the olive oil, yoghurt and mint in a medium bowl. Season with salt and pepper and set aside.

Peel and slice the onions and garlic. Peel the potatoes and cut into large chunks.

Put the meat, garlic, cumin and curry powder in a medium bowl. Season with salt and pepper and combine using your hands. Shape into meatballs the size of a small egg. Set aside on a plate.

Heat the olive oil in a tagine over medium–high heat. Add the meatballs and cook on all sides, turning them gently. Add the onions, potato, honey and thyme and cook, stirring, until beginning to brown. Add 150 ml (5 fl oz) water and season with salt and pepper. Reduce the heat to low, cover and simmer for 45 minutes.

Adjust the seasoning and serve.

Suggestion
Serve hot with a green salad and the mint yoghurt sauce.

BÚN BÒ WITH SLICED BEEF, LETTUCE AND CHIPS

Serves 4–6

3 garlic cloves

30 g (1 oz) ginger

1 handful coriander (cilantro)

12 lettuce leaves

800 g (1 lb 12 oz) inside round steak ('round petite tender')

3 tablespoons soy sauce

4 tablespoons olive oil

4 servings crispy potato chips (p. 238)

Preparation time
30 minutes

Resting time
3 hours

Cooking time
10 minutes

Peel and chop the garlic and ginger. Pick and wash the coriander leaves. Wash the lettuce leaves, remove any tough parts and slice.

Cut the meat into thin slices and place in a medium bowl with the garlic, ginger and soy sauce. Cover and set aside in the refrigerator for 3 hours.

Five minutes before serving time, heat the olive oil in a large frying pan over high heat. Add the meat with its marinade and cook, stirring constantly, for 5–8 minutes. Divide the lettuce, coriander and crispy potato chips between four large serving bowls. Place the meat on top of the lettuce, toss gently and serve.

Food and wine pairings

Family-style beef stew (p. 60)
> Givry red, Côte de Beaune

Alsatian beef and potato casserole (p. 384)
> Alsace pinot noir, Bourgogne Passe-Tout-Grains,
> Saumur-Champigny, Saint-Amour

Flank steak with caramelised shallots (p. 40)
> Bordeaux, Bordeaux supérieur,
> Côtes de Blaye, Lussac-Saint-Émilion,
> Puisseguin-Saint-Émilion, Graves

Rolled steak and cheese (p. 90)
> Saumur-Champigny, Bordeaux supérieur, Faugères,
> Saint-Chinian, Minervois, Crozes-Hermitage

Poached beef with vegetables (p. 98)
> Irancy, Monthélie, Pernand-Vergelesses,
> Savigny-lès-Beaune, Coteaux-Champenois

Beef bourguignon (p. 32)
Braised beef and carrots (p. 130)
> Côte de Beaune-Villages, Côte de Nuits-Villages,
> Maranges, Ladoix, Fixin

Meatballs in tomato and capsicum sauce (p. 42)
> Fitou, Corbières-Boutenac,
> Côtes-du-Roussillon-Villages, Luberon,
> Costières de Nîmes

Beef, capsicum and anchovy skewers (p. 22)
> Buzet, Listrac-Médoc, Anjou-Villages,
> Bourgueil, Fronton

Belgian beef and beer stew (p. 76)
> Bourgogne Côte-Chalonnaise,
> Côte de Nuits-Villages,
> Aloxe-Corton, Saumur-Champigny, Bourgueil

Spicy dry beef curry (p. 46)
> Tavel, Bandol, Côtes du Rhône, Ventoux,
> Côtes du Vivarais

Chilli con carne (p. 186)
> Alsace pinot noir, Côtes du Rhône, Morgon,
> Saumur-Champigny

Pepper steak (p. 152)
> Margaux, Saint-Julien, Saint-Émilion Grand Cru,
> Pessac-Léognan, Gevrey-Chambertin, Chambertin,
> Chambertin-Clos-de-Bèze

Rib steak with crispy onions (p. 212)
Marinated and grilled rib steak (p. 18)
> Margaux, Saint-Julien, Pauillac, Saint-Estèphe,
> Pessac-Léognan, Hermitage, Côte-Rôtie, Corton,
> Chambolle-Musigny

Indian-style beef curry (p. 170)
> Minervois-La Livinière, Cornas, Crozes-Hermitage,
> Saint-Joseph, Pierrevert

Beef stew with olives and orange (p.180)
> Blaye-Côtes de Bordeaux, Côtes de Bourg,
> Patrimonio, Lirac, Gevrey-Chambertin

Provençal beef stew with chickpea chips (p. 88)
> Côtes de Provence, Coteaux Varois-en-Provence,
> Bandol, Ajaccio, Lirac, Côtes du Rhône-Villages

Beef cheeks braised in red wine (p. 210)
> Listrac-Médoc, Cadillac-Côtes de Bordeaux,
> Luberon, Gigondas, Vinsobres

Beef and chilli empanadas (p. 84)
> Languedoc, Costières de Nîmes,
> Côtes du Rhône-Villages, Fitou, Cabardès,
> Languedoc

Beef and wheat berry stir-fry with Thai basil (p. 52)
Beef stir-fry with Thai basil (p. 100)
Beef stir-fry with roasted peanuts (p. 226)
Bún bò with sliced beef, lettuce and chips (p. 400)
Sautéed beef with minted peas (p. 94)
> Côtes de Provence, Coteaux-Varois-en-Provence, Tavel, Cabardès

Rib eye steak with red wine sauce (p. 26)
> Saint-Émilion, Sainte-Foy-Bordeaux, Castillon-Côtes de Bordeaux, Blaye-Côtes de Bordeaux, Canon-Fronsac

Sautéed beef with mushrooms (p. 20)
> Graves, Lalande-de-Pomerol, Fronsac, Médoc, Saint-Émilion, Chinon, Saint-Sardos, Madiran

Roast beef with béarnaise sauce (p. 48)
> Bordeaux, Bordeaux supérieur, Côtes de Bourg, Sainte-Foy-Bordeaux, Chorey-lès-Beaune

Chilli beef and capsicum fajitas (p. 92)
Striploin steak with bay leaf and curry oil (p. 200)
> Canon-Fronsac, Francs-Côtes-de-Bordeaux, Saint-Émilion, Saint-Georges-Saint-Émilion, Saint-Sardos, Tursan

Beef wellington (p. 350)
> Romanée, Vosne-Romanée, Gevrey-Chambertin, Pomerol, Saint-Émilion Grand Cru, Pessac-Léognan, Margaux, Saint-Julien, Cornas, Hermitage, Côte-Rôtie

Beef stew with olives and bacon (p. 206)
> Bandol, Côtes de Provence, Palette, Costières de Nîmes, Vacqueyras, Lirac, Côtes du Rhône-Villages

Koftas with spices, coriander and rocket (p. 124)
> Fitou, Côtes du Roussillon, Tavel

Beef stew with spring vegetables (p. 184)
Hanger steak with caramelised baby onions (p. 166)
> Chinon, Saint-Nicolas-de-Bourgueil, Saumur-Champigny, Fleurie, Castillon-Côtes de Bordeaux

Roquefort steak (p. 106)
> Bordeaux supérieur, Cahors, Béarn, Madiran, Tursan

Pot-au-feu with purple potatoes (p. 364)
> Beaujolais-Villages, Brouilly, Saint-Nicolas-de-Bourgueil, Anjou-Villages, Côte de Nuits-Villages

Braised oxtail with red wine (p. 162)
> Anjou-Gamay, Touraine (gamay), Coteaux du Lyonnais, Saint-Amour (beaujolais), Régnié, Côte Roannaise, Côtes d'Auvergne

Grilled steak with herb and watercress sauce (p. 74)
> Bordeaux, Bordeaux supérieur, Blaye, Côtes du Rhône-Villages, Fronton, Buzet, Beaujolais-Villages

Beef and potato tagine (p. 398)
> Faugères, Fitou, Côtes du Rhône-Villages, Collioure, Côtes du Roussillon-Villages

Classic steak tartare (p. 188)
> Côtes de Bourg, Fronton, Côtes du Marmandais, Malepère, Beaujolais, Coteaux du Lyonnais, Côte Roannaise, Côtes du Vivarais, Côtes du Rhône

Fillet steak with truffles and foie gras (p. 28)
> Anjou-Villages Brissac, Fitou, Pomerol, Saint-Émilion Grand Cru, Haut-Médoc

Beef and onion stir-fry (p. 222)
> Côtes de Provence, Coteaux-Varois-en-Provence, Tavel, Cabardès, Fleurie, Chiroubles, Anjou-Gamay

Recipe index

POTATOES

BEEF & POTATOES

I would like to thank the butchers and potato farmers who warmly welcomed me into their workplaces so I could create this book.

The Duciel family Boucherie Pascal Duciel
41 Avenue de Saxe 75007 Paris

Yves-Marie Le Bourdonnec
'The bohemian butcher'

Boucherie Lamartine
172 Avenue Victor-Hugo 75016 Paris

Magalie Bars 'The potato bar'
Selling potatoes at the Avenue de Saxe market in the 7th arrondissement, Paris, on Thursday and Saturday mornings, and also at the Auguste-Blanqui market in the 13th arrondissement on Sunday mornings.

Philippe Morice
Market gardener at the Avenue de Saxe market in the 7th arrondissement, Paris, on Thursday and Saturday mornings, and also at the Auguste-Blanqui market in the 13th arrondissement on Sunday mornings.

I would also like to thank Catherine Saunier-Talec, Valérie Ballot and Antoine Béon, who came up with the idea of this book with me over a lunch of steak and chips.

And also Juliette Spiteri for her efficient coordination.

Published in 2016 by Murdoch Books,
   an imprint of Allen & Unwin
First published by Hachette Livre (Hachette Pratique),
   Paris, in 2014

Murdoch Books Australia
83 Alexander Street
Crows Nest NSW 2065
Phone: +61 (0) 2 8425 0100
Fax: +61 (0) 2 9906 2218
murdochbooks.com.au
info@murdochbooks.com.au

Murdoch Books UK
Ormond House
26–27 Boswell Street
London WC1N 3JZ
Phone: +44 (0) 20 8785 5995
murdochbooks.co.uk
info@murdochbooks.co.uk

For Corporate Orders & Custom Publishing, contact our Business Development Team at salesenquiries@murdochbooks.com.au.

Publisher: Corinne Roberts
Manager: Catherine Saunier-Talec
Editorial manager: Céline Le Lamer
Editor: Juliette Spiteri
Art director: Antoine Béon
Graphic design: Marie-Paule Jaulme
Introductory texts: Emmanuelle Jary
Translator: Melissa McMahon
Production Manager: Alexandra Gonzalez

A cataloguing-in-publication entry is available from the catalogue of the National Library of Australia at nla.gov.au.

ISBN 978 1 74336 628 8 Australia
ISBN 978 1 74336 629 5 UK

A catalogue record for this book is available from the British Library.

Colour reproduction: Splitting Image Colour Studio Pty Ltd
Printed by 1010 Printing International Limited, China

IMPORTANT: Those who might be at risk from the effects of salmonella poisoning (the elderly, pregnant women, young children and those suffering from immune deficiency diseases) should consult their doctor with any concerns about eating raw eggs and raw beef.

OVEN GUIDE: You may find cooking times vary depending on the oven you are using. For fan-forced ovens, as a general rule, set the oven temperature to 20°C (35°F) lower than indicated in the recipe.

MEASURES GUIDE: We have used 15 ml (3 teaspoon) tablespoon measures.